**Lampshades
Technique
and Design**

Making Lampshades

Angela Fishburn

Drake Publishers Inc.
New York · London

For Sarah

Published in 1975 by
Drake Publishers Inc.
381 Park Avenue South
New York, N.Y. 10016

ISBN: 0-87749-844-X

Printed in Great Britain

Contents

Introduction

Lampshade making can be a very absorbing and interesting hobby — a creative and enjoyable craft which is relatively inexpensive. It is immensely satisfying to produce a lampshade of your own choice and colour and perhaps even of your own design. Commercially produced lampshades can be very expensive and often it is hard to find exact requirements. Couture shades which are made by hand can be made to order but are very costly.

Lampshade making provides an opportunity for the expert needlewoman or artist to use her other skills, for example, macramé, patchwork, lacemaking, linen embroidery and other modern crafts, as well as oil painting, appliqué and fabric printing. The limits are endless for those who are ingenious and would like to combine these and other skills.

Making lampshades covers a wide range of materials and shapes — from raffia to the most elegant of silk shades with exotic designs. In this book, however, I have tried to give instructions for making the type of lampshades that I should find acceptable in my own home and ones that I hope you would like to see in yours too. With a little patience and practice it is a skill which I think is well worth acquiring, both from the aesthetic and practical point of view.

1 Design and colour

Design

Lampshades play an important part in the décor of our homes — they are both functional and decorative. As they are comparatively cheap and easy to make they are probably changed more frequently than most other soft furnishings. There is, however, more to making a lampshade than just covering the frame. There are many methods of doing this, but before deciding which one to choose there are various points to bear in mind:

1 A lampshade can be an important focal point in a room as it can give a splash of colour in a dark corner, or provide impact in an otherwise neutral-toned room.
2 Do not always choose a lampshade for the effect it gives at night — remember that it must also fit into the décor during the day when it is not lit.
3 Fashions in lampshades are always changing: fresh designs in frames are always being introduced and new colours used. Develop design and colour sense by looking at glossy magazines and shop displays. Learn to appreciate and recognize good design. Look round the large stores and hunt out the good interior decorator shops and make a note of any interesting detail. This is time well spent

and will help to develop an appreciation of colour and design.
4 A room can be transformed and given a new lease of life with a new lampshade carefully chosen and made in an up to the minute design and colour.

Colour

Colour has great power and reflects the personality as is shown in the colours different types of people choose to wear. This also applies in the home too, and different colours reflect different moods. Similarly, with lampshades, some colours are thought more suitable than others.

Remember that lighting at night will change the overall tone of the room, and it is therefore important to position lamps in the most advantageous way. Diagrams 1 and 2 show how different positioning of the lights can affect the overall tone of the room. This can be changed even more by the choice of lampshade colour and can be quite dramatic.

It is usually more effective to have several lamps in a room rather than one central light. Having several pools of light shining up or down rather than one central light makes the scheme more interesting.

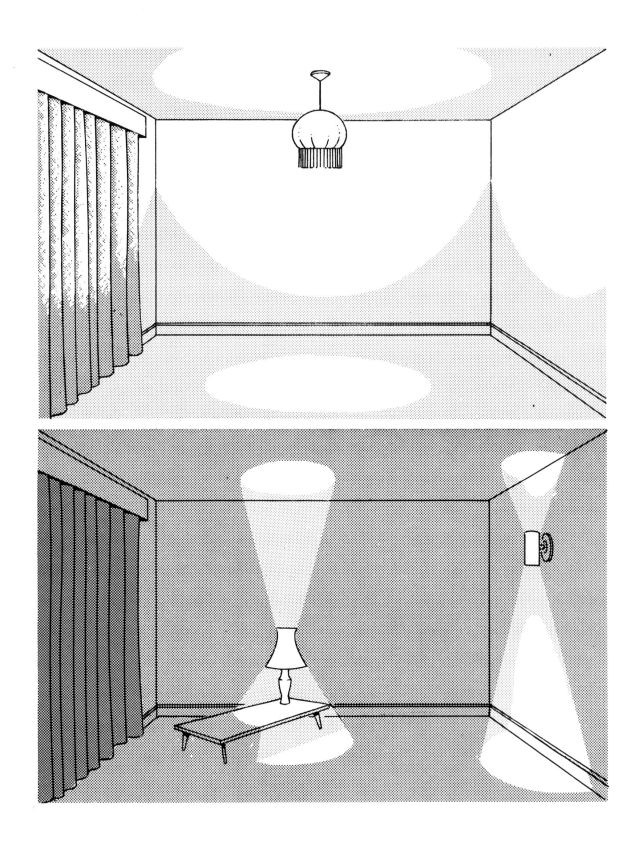

Always keep a naked bulb covered, except in the case of low-wattage candle bulbs and chandelier-type fittings. With the latter, a clear bulb should be used and not a pearl one, as this spoils the effect of the crystal in the chandelier.

Beware of using patterned material for lamp-shades as this can detract from the fabrics of the other soft furnishings. Too much pattern in a room makes it look busy and it is often better to keep the lampshades of plain or textured fabric, keeping a tailored and uncluttered look. Be wary also of using fussy trimmings. Often a shade looks far more effective with a plain trimming and can be spoilt by a fancy one.

Fabrics

Before choosing fabric for a lampshade, collect samples and cuttings in various colours and textures. Experiment with them in different combinations to see if they either tone or contrast well with the rest of the room setting. Build up a collection for future reference.

Always test the fabric over a lighted bulb to see the effect it will produce. If possible try the lining material also, because this can change the colour of the outer fabric. A white lining reflects the maximum amount of light but does not change the colour of the outer fabric. A coloured lining changes the tone of the outer fabric and may be disappointing. However, a peach or pink lining can add warmth to an otherwise cool colour.

When choosing fabric remember that colour can create illusions of shape and can affect the illusion of the lampshade's size. If a pale colour is used this will make the shade appear larger, but a dark colour will make the shade appear smaller (diagram 3).

Train the eye by constantly looking at good design and try to develop awareness of current trends in colour combinations. Collect pictures and ideas and stick them in a scrapbook for reference. This is invaluable for ideas which may otherwise be lost or forgotten. (Choice of fabrics is discussed on page 27 and page 78.)

Opposite
1 Central lighting illuminates the whole room but makes shadows
2 Local light gives strong shadow and can create interest in a small area

3 A shade of the same size produces the illusion of being bigger or smaller, depending on a light or dark shade

2 Choosing a base

The choice of a suitable base is very important, and considerable thought should be given to this. If possible take the base to the shop when choosing a frame to see that the proportion and balance are right — in other words 'does it satisfy the eye?'. This is discussed more fully on page 14.

A large selection of bases is available in all sorts of shapes and sizes, some good, many bad. Some bases tip over easily and are therefore not practical. Be selective and choose a solid base, one that is not too light in weight.

If possible, buy the base first and then choose a lampshade to suit it — not the other way round. This is because it is often easier to carry a base to a shop than to take a large lampshade which might easily get damaged in the process.

Look out for good Spanish ceramic and Italian alabaster bases and also plain bases with simple modern lines. Avoid fussy bases with too much detail that detracts from the lampshade. There are many brass, alabaster and ceramic bases from which to choose in most of the large stores.

It is often possible to find lovely old vases in local junk shops. These can be converted into very suitable bases. Old brass and silver candlesticks also make very elegant bases, and reproduction ones are available at many stores. The cost of converting candlesticks or vases varies from £3.00 upwards depending on the method and materials used.

It is seldom worth using wine decanters and bottles for lamp bases — they were not designed for this purpose and are seldom enhanced by being converted. They are not usually of the correct proportions to be used for bases (see diagram 4). Acid carboys, however, can make attractive bases for larger shades and can be used in combination with pebbles, etc.

*4 (a) Bottles used as bases: the shades do not balance well
        with the bases
   (b) Vase used as base: a much better balance is achieved*

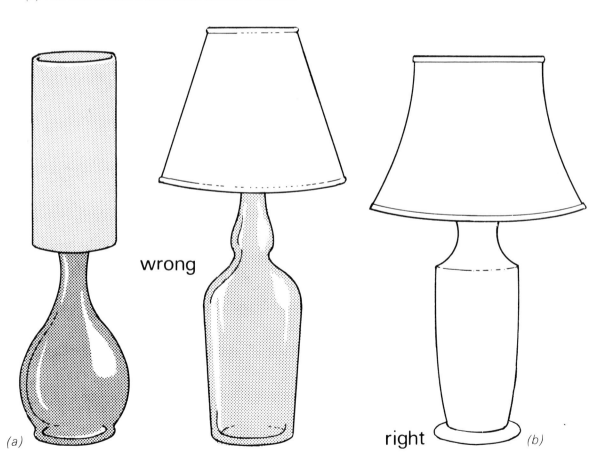

wrong

right

(a)

(b)

3 Choosing a frame

Having chosen the base, think about the lamp-shade frame. Bear in mind the purpose for which the light is intended – is it for background lighting (indirect), reading (direct), or diffused (coming through silk or other fabric)?

Make sure the right size of shade is chosen for the light required. A hanging or pendant light is usually positioned where the light is needed, for example in a hall or landing, so make sure that the bottom of the shade is large enough to enable the light to spread. If the light is too glaring use a louvre attachment to diffuse it. A louvre can be clipped into the bottom ring of most shades (see page 22).

Consider the height of the ceilings and the colour of the walls – remembering that pale colours on walls reflect more light than dark ones. Wall lights reflect the light on to the walls and back into the room and so can give considerable light if the walls are pale.

When choosing a frame for a lamp base it is often difficult to know how large or small the shade should be. There are no hard and fast rules about this but as a general guide the shade should be about the same height as the base, with slight variations either way depending on the design of the base and frame. There is no rule for the width of the shade, but the best way of deciding is by constantly looking at pictures and displays to see what the eye finds pleasing. Alternatively, draw various shapes of bases on card and cut out basic shapes in paper representing shades. Try these on the bases and experiment with bases and shades until a suitable one is found (diagram 6). When doing this it will be found that some lampshade frames are more adaptable than others. For example, a cone shade will fit almost any base whereas with other shapes it is necessary to choose the base carefully and balance shade to base, keeping in mind the design of both. If the shade is chosen with care, relating the size and design to the base, the overall effect can be most rewarding and pleasing results can be achieved.

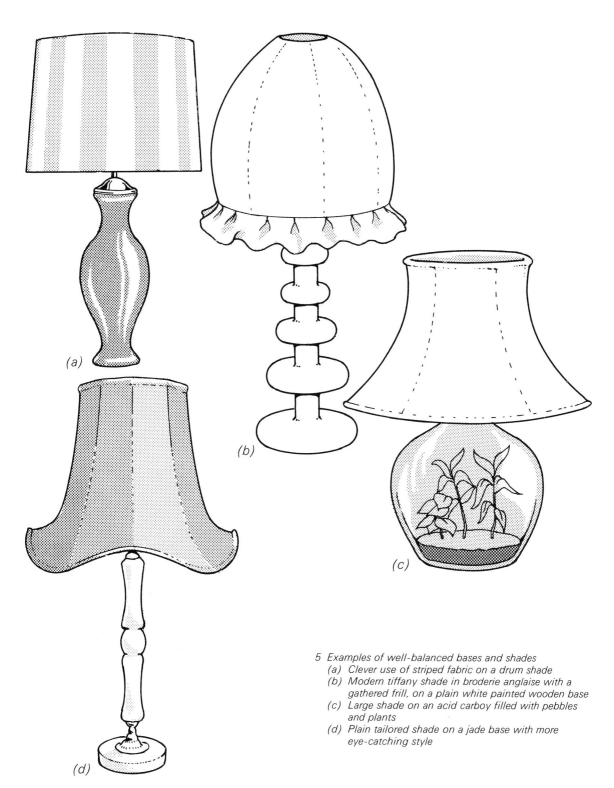

(a)

(b)

(c)

(d)

5 Examples of well-balanced bases and shades
  (a) Clever use of striped fabric on a drum shade
  (b) Modern tiffany shade in broderie anglaise with a
      gathered frill, on a plain white painted wooden base
  (c) Large shade on an acid carboy filled with pebbles
      and plants
  (d) Plain tailored shade on a jade base with more
      eye-catching style

(e) Unusual shade on a base which complements the
    design of the shade
(f) Curved empire shade with 'collar' at the bottom edge
(g) Waisted shade used with a converted brass candlestick
(h) Panelled shade used with a converted vase

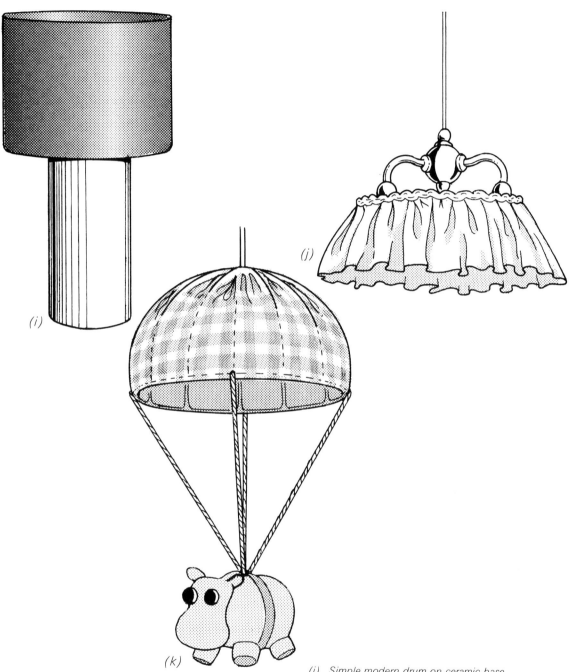

(i)

(j)

(k)

(i) Simple modern drum on ceramic base
(j) A pendant fitting with a gathered shade
(k) A nursery shade: a 'parachute' made from gingham,
     with thick piping cord used to fix a pretty soft toy
     at the bottom

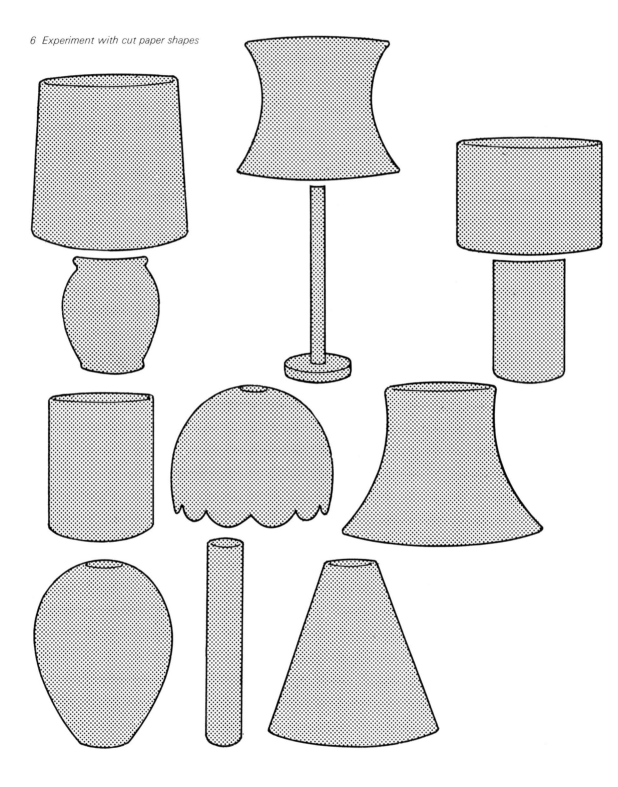

4 Frames and fittings

The frame and fitting is the first and most important consideration when making a lampshade. This is the foundation of a successful shade.

Lampshade frames are usually made from copper or galvanized steel wires. They are obtainable in a very large range of sizes and shapes, from candle shades to large standard lampshades, and new ones are always being introduced. A good frame will be made of a suitable thickness or gauge of wire for the size of the frame. The best frames have soldered wires, but most are spot welded, so it is wise to check that the joints are firm and strong. A badly made frame can spoil a lampshade. Frames can become badly bent and out of shape while lying in a shop, so check that the frame is not distorted in any way. It is very difficult to remedy a fault like this. Often a badly made lampshade is the result of a faulty frame.

If the required shape is not available it is often possible to get a lampshade frame specially made to order (see names and addresses on page 89). This is particularly useful if an unusual shape is required, and it can be fun to design a lampshade especially for a particular base.

It is advisable to paint the frame with a good, quick-drying enamel paint (allowing a day or two to dry thoroughly) as this reduces the risk of the frame rusting when the lampshade is washed. It also helps in the case of condensation, or in an area close to the sea.

Frames are made for use with various different kinds of fittings. Make sure that the frame has the correct fitting for the light. The diagrams show some of the shapes available and illustrate the different fittings.

Always file down any rough edges at the joints of the struts, as these may push through the binding tape and fabric.

It is not usually worth using an old frame unless it is a particularly well-made one. Frames often get distorted and out of shape over the years and frequently show signs of rust. As a rule it is wiser to invest in a fresh frame. However, if a favourite old frame is being used, take off the old binding tape and check for rust. File off any apparent rust and paint with gloss paint, checking that the frame is not distorted in any way. Tape in the usual way (see page 30).

Frames are made in sizes from 7·6–10·2 cm (3–4 in.) for small wall lights, up to 50·8–55·8 cm (20–22 in.) for large standard lamps. This measurement is taken across the diameter of the base ring of the frame (diagram 26).

Plastic-coated frames are also available, but

19

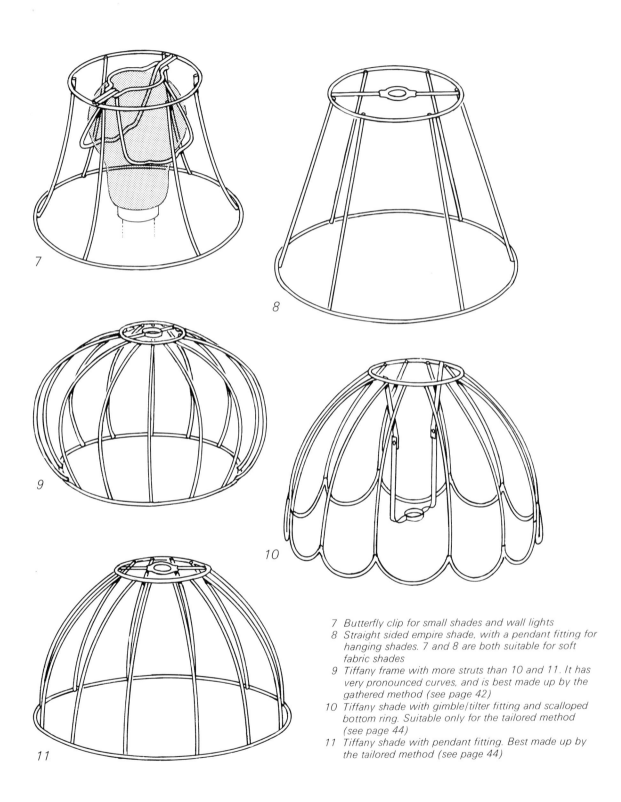

7 Butterfly clip for small shades and wall lights
8 Straight sided empire shade, with a pendant fitting for
   hanging shades. 7 and 8 are both suitable for soft
   fabric shades
9 Tiffany frame with more struts than 10 and 11. It has
   very pronounced curves, and is best made up by the
   gathered method (see page 42)
10 Tiffany shade with gimble/tilter fitting and scalloped
   bottom ring. Suitable only for the tailored method
   (see page 44)
11 Tiffany shade with pendant fitting. Best made up by
   the tailored method (see page 44)

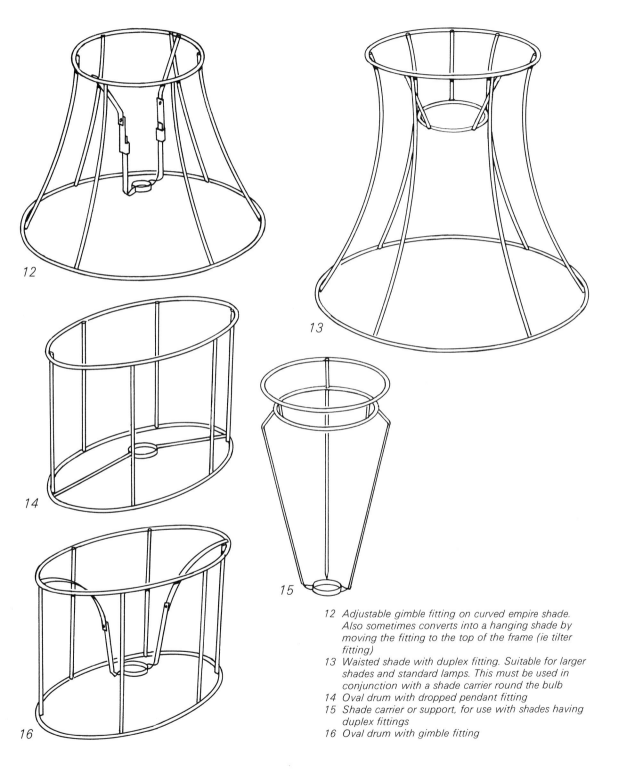

12 Adjustable gimble fitting on curved empire shade.
   Also sometimes converts into a hanging shade by
   moving the fitting to the top of the frame (ie tilter
   fitting)
13 Waisted shade with duplex fitting. Suitable for larger
   shades and standard lamps. This must be used in
   conjunction with a shade carrier round the bulb
14 Oval drum with dropped pendant fitting
15 Shade carrier or support, for use with shades having
   duplex fittings
16 Oval drum with gimble fitting

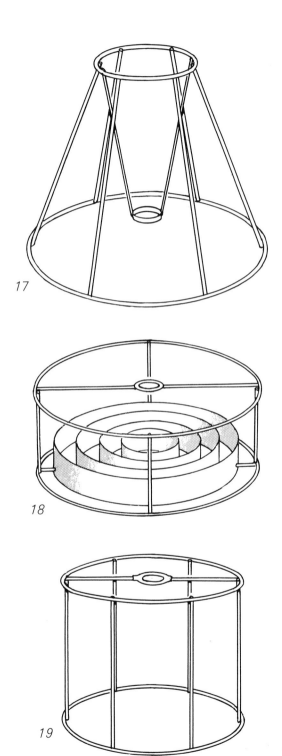

these are more costly. However, these are seldom worth the extra expense and have the disadvantage that the wires are rather more bulky than necessary because of the plastic coating. It is preferable to paint an ordinary frame with gloss or enamel paint.

Lampshades fall into two groups — soft fabric shades and firm rigid ones. Different techniques are used for making these and it is therefore important to have some knowledge of the frames and fabrics used for each group.

Soft fabric lampshades

These are made from flexible materials — silks, satins, lawns, chiffons, etc. It is necessary to make these on frames that have struts as well as a ring at the top and bottom, for this gives the frame its shape. The size of the frame, therefore, cannot be varied as with a firm shade. These shades can be washed, providing suitable fabric is chosen (see chapter 6, page 26).

Firm shades

These are made from stiff or rigid materials such as buckram, parchment and covered card. Many ready-made materials are available from good handicraft shops, but it is also possible to make suitable material at home using *Selapar* or *Parbond*.

When making a firm shade, a ring set is used. This consists of a top and bottom ring with an appropriate fitting. Strutted frames are not essential for making firm shades as the rigid material forms the shape of the shade, although they can, of course, be used if desired.

Firm shades are quick and easy to make and can be made with the minimum of effort. Some firm lampshades can be washed but most can only be brushed or wiped over, depending on the material used.

17 *Cone shape with gimble fitting*
18 *Drum shape using louvre to diffuse light. Leave at least 2·5 cm (1 in.) between the bulb and louvre fitting*
19 *Drum shape with pendant fitting*

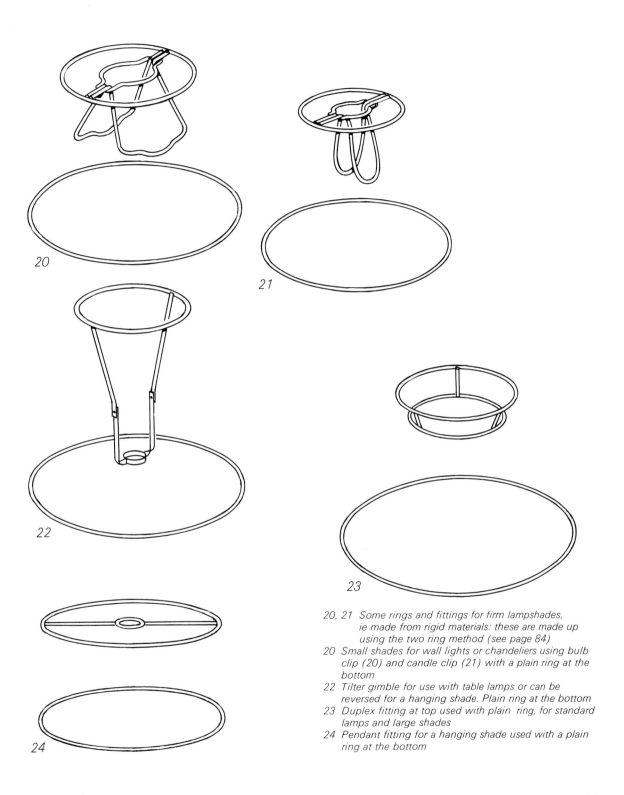

20, 21 Some rings and fittings for firm lampshades,
ie made from rigid materials: these are made up
using the two ring method (see page 84)
20 Small shades for wall lights or chandeliers using bulb
clip (20) and candle clip (21) with a plain ring at the
bottom
22 Tilter gimble for use with table lamps or can be
reversed for a hanging shade. Plain ring at the bottom
23 Duplex fitting at top used with plain ring, for standard
lamps and large shades
24 Pendant fitting for a hanging shade used with a plain
ring at the bottom

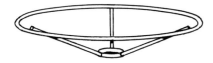

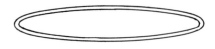

25(a)

(b)

25 Dropped pendant fitting used with a plain ring.
   Suitable for a hanging shade or can be reversed and
   used on a lamp base with the plain ring at the top
26 Taking a measurement for the diameter of a frame

26

5 Tools and equipment

To make lampshades successfully does not require any specialized equipment but this is a list of the basic tools which are necessary:

1 Sharp pair of scissors, one for cutting fabric and a smaller pair for trimming seams, etc.

2 Needles — Sharps 3/9 for making soft fabric shades. Betweens 5/6 for firm shades.

3 Steel dressmaking pins. Pinning correctly is a very important part of making lampshades. Badly placed pins can tear the fabric and make marks that cannot easily be removed. Invest in a new packet or tin of best steel dressmaking pins and do not use any that are at all rusty. These will leave permanent marks on the fabric. Never use pins that have dropped on to the floor — they collect dust that is not visible to the naked eye. Glass-headed pins can be used, but extra care is needed when using these as they are very sharp.

If a finger is pricked and blood accidentally gets on to the lampshade fabric the best way to remove it is to chew a piece of ordinary tacking cotton and rub it on to the bloodstain. This removes the stain without leaving a water mark.

4 Good adhesive. *UHU* is the most satisfactory glue for lampshade making. It is used when making firm lampshades and also when applying certain trimmings to soft fabric shades where stitching is not satisfactory.

5 1·3 cm ($\frac{1}{2}$ in.) wide lampshade tape or soft cotton tape for binding the frame.

6 Thimble.

7 Matching silk.

8 Spring clothes pegs (preferably wooden) for making firm shades.

9 Lampshade frame (see chapter 4).

10 Fabric to cover the frame (see chapters 7 and 16).

11 Trimmings. There are many good commercially made trimmings available. It is also possible to make hand-made trimmings and these can be most effective. Beware of using trimmings that are too fussy. (See chapter 15).

6 Care of lampshades

To keep lampshades looking fresh and clean, brush regularly with a soft brush, making sure that the trimming is treated carefully. Most soft fabric lampshades, including pleated and swathed shades can be washed when necessary, if a little care is taken.

It is essential that the shade is dried as quickly as possible to avoid rust forming on the frame, so choose a warm windy day, swish the lampshade in warm water with a mild detergent, rinse and hang on the line to drip dry. When dry put in an airing cupboard, if possible, for 24 hours. If a contrasting coloured trimming has been used check the colour fastness of this, as it could run and ruin the shade. Washing can sometimes improve a shade that is loose and baggy, as the material tends to shrink and makes the lampshade tighter.

As most firm or rigid shades cannot be washed they should be kept clean by regular brushing or use of a vacuum cleaner. Some can be sponged clean, but this depends on the fabric used.

Soft Fabric Lampshades

7 Choice of fabrics for cover and lining

Cover materials

There are so many dress and furnishing fabrics on the market that are suitable for making lampshades that there is really no limit to the choice. However, here are a few points to bear in mind when choosing cover materials.

(a) Choose fabric that has plenty of elasticity or 'give' and therefore one that will mould easily to the shape of the lampshade frame. This is particularly important in the case of a curved empire shape, which needs fabric that will stretch over the frame without wrinkling. Stiff, non-stretchy fabrics are not suitable for curved frames.

(b) When making a pleated or swathed lampshade, choose material with good draping qualities, such as silk chiffon or georgette. Nylon chiffon is not suitable as it does not pleat well and is too springy.

(c) Some materials are not enhanced when put over a light, eg brocade and some heavy furnishing fabrics, so test these before deciding to buy them.

(d) Beware of using striped material for lampshades. It can be exceedingly difficult to match the stripes, except when used for a hard drum shade or positioned diagonally.

(e) Fabrics which split and tear easily are not suitable: for example, taffeta and rayon satin linings. They show all pin marks and do not wash well.

(f) If possible choose a fabric that has good washing qualities. The lampshade can then be washed frequently which is particularly important if it is white or light in colour.

(g) When choosing patterned fabrics (eg for a tiffany shade) remember that small patterns look more effective than larger ones.

(h) Heavy furnishing fabrics, heavy cottons, nylon and materials that do not stretch well, are not generally suitable.

(i) Colours: Any colour is acceptable providing it fits into the colour scheme of the room, but some colours give a more attractive light than others. Good colours include tones of gold, red and green. Dead white shades give a cold light, but give a warmer light if lined with pink or peach. Blue shades transmit a cold light; brown can be most effective, but can give a dingy light, so care is needed when using it.

Fabrics

1 Crêpe-backed satin: a good choice for the beginner as well as the more experienced worker, as it is the easiest of all to use. It has plenty of 'give', is reasonably priced and

comes in a good range of colours. It can be used for the cover of the lampshade as well as for the lining. It looks well used either on the crêpe or on the satin side. It is particularly useful for curved shapes and for all linings.

2 Rayon dupion: more difficult to use, but has an attractive grain in the fabric which looks effective when the lampshade is lit. Available in a good range of colours and is reasonably priced. Suitable for all shapes of shades.

3 Taiho, *Tricel* and other man-made fabrics: some of these can be used successfully for lampshade covers, but are not suitable for linings, as they lack elasticity. However, new fabrics are always being introduced and it is as well to experiment with these. They are reasonably priced and usually wash well.

4 Jap silk: although a suitable fabric for smaller shades, it is not very easy to use on larger ones. It tends to pin-mark easily and can split if great care is not taken. Suitable for lining small shades, it washes well and is reasonably priced.

5 Silk shantung: very suitable fabric for both outer cover and lining, produced in a good range of subtle colours. Reasonably priced and washes well.

6 Wild Thai silk: the most luxurious of all fabrics for making lampshades. It is more costly than most others, but has a most attractive grain and shimmer which other materials lack. As this fabric dyes so well it is possible to buy a very wide range of subtle colours which are extremely suitable for lampshades. It is strong, durable, easy to work and washes well. Suitable for all types of lampshades from small wall lights to large standard shades.

7 Silk chiffon and georgette: the best choice of fabric for pleated and swathed lampshades. It has very good draping qualities and retains pleating well, unlike nylon chiffon, which is not suitable as the pleating does not lie flat, or 'set' well. Silk chiffon and georgette is available in a very wide range of subtle and bright colours, and washes extremely well.

8 Light dress cottons (fine lawns, broderie anglaise, gingham): all make delightful covers for many lampshades. There is such a range of interesting patterns and colours that the choice is limitless. These fabrics, however, are not so suitable for making Empire-shaped shades as they are not usually flexible enough and do not stretch well. They are, however, suitable for straight-sided frames, firm shades and lampshades made by the sectional method (see chapter 13), as well as tiffany shades of all types.

Linings

The purpose of a lining is:

(a) To hide the struts, particularly in a pendant (hanging) shade.

(b) To avoid the bulb showing through the cover material and to give body to the shade when using light-weight fabrics such as pure silk, chiffon and georgette.

(c) To reflect as much light as possible. A white lining reflects the maximum amount of light and is a good choice when the cover material is dark.

(d) To obtain different effects when using coloured linings. For example a peach or pink lining gives a warm glow to a white cover.

There are two main methods of lining lampshades.

(a) Balloon lining: This is fitted inside the struts on the inside of the frame and needs practice to make perfect. It is fitted after the cover has been sewn to the outside of the frame. This type of lining is used where possible as it hides all the struts. However, it is not possible to use this lining on all frames, eg tiffany and square frames. These should have an external lining or a lining made using the sectional method (see chapter 13).

(b) External lining: This is fitted on to the outer side of the struts where a balloon lining is not practical. This applies to small chandelier type shades and small wall lights where a balloon lining would be too near to the bulb. An external lining is also used on square frames as a balloon lining cannot be fitted successfully on these because of the shape of the frame. A slight variation of this lining is used when making pleated and swathed lampshades (see chapter 12).

Lining materials

The fabric for a lining should be strong but light-weight, and should not fray easily or pin-mark. Crêpe-back satin is the best choice as it has plenty of give, is reasonable in price and has a shiny surface which reflects the light well. Jap silk is only suitable for small shades and is not as easy to use as crêpe-back satin. Do not use taffeta or rayon satin lining material, as these split and pin mark badly.

All lampshades are enhanced by a lining.

8 Taping the frame

Every lampshade needs to be bound with tape to give a firm foundation for the stitching and pinning. It also helps to prevent rust from forming.

Great care should be taken when taping because although it is perhaps the least interesting part of making a lampshade, it is a vital process which needs to be mastered. If it is not done with care a disappointing result will be achieved and the finished shade will be loose and baggy instead of firm and taut. The tape must be tight and smooth on the struts and rings. To test whether it is tight enough try twisting it round with the fingers. If it moves at all it means that it is not sufficiently tight and needs to be re-bound. The cover and lining will slip if sewn to a loose binding and this will result in a baggy lampshade. It is well worth the effort of re-taping a loosely bound shade.

1 Use 1·3 cm ($\frac{1}{2}$ in.) wide lampshade tape or soft cotton tape. This is a poor quality tape which is loosely woven and off-white in colour. It is easily dyed with a home dye to the colour of the lining, if necessary. This is sometimes useful when an external lining is being used and the struts are showing, eg with a tiffany shade.

2 *Paris binding:* This can be used for binding the frame when the colour of the binding is important and when the struts show. Available in a good range of colours.

3 *Jap silk:* Can be used to bind the struts. Gives a smooth finish. Cut into 2·5 cm (1 in.) strips and turn in one raw edge as the strut is bound. Lampshade tape, however, must be used on any struts where sewing or pinning will take place, that is, round the top and bottom rings and down each side strut, as it is not possible to sew or pin on to a strut bound with Jap silk.

4 *Bias binding:* Comes in a good range of colours. Iron one side open to prevent it from being too bulky.

Quantity of tape

For the struts allow roughly $1\frac{1}{2}$ times the length of each strut. Do not allow more than this or the tape will be too bulky.

For the top and bottom rings allow twice the circumference. More is needed for the rings because the tape is bound round each join of strut and ring.

Method

Tape each strut separately and then tape the top

and bottom rings. Always start and finish at a join in the strut and ring otherwise the binding may work loose. No sewing is necessary except when taping rings for firm lampshades where there are no struts. In this case use a small piece of *Sellotape* (sticky tape) to hold the tape in position when starting. Finish by sewing on the outside of the ring, so that when the fabric is placed on the ring it hides the stitches (diagram 27).

1 Trim end of tape and place under ring, starting at the top of the frame. Tuck in and wind tape round the strut just overlapping the tape. This is done at rather an acute angle, and is helped if a slight pull is given at each time round. This stretches the tape slightly and makes it mould to the strut more easily. Keep the tape smooth and very tight and avoid any ridges that tend to appear (diagrams 28, 29, 30).

27 Stitches on outer edge of ring to finish off taping

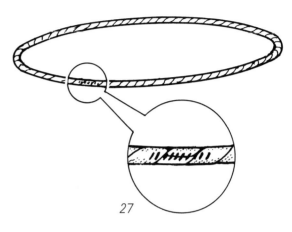

27

28–30 Stages in taping the struts

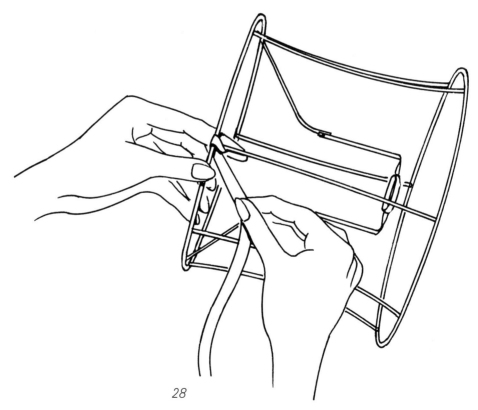

28

31 *Turning lampshade to new position for taping bottom ring*

The scalloped top of this lampshade balances well with the urn shaped alabaster base

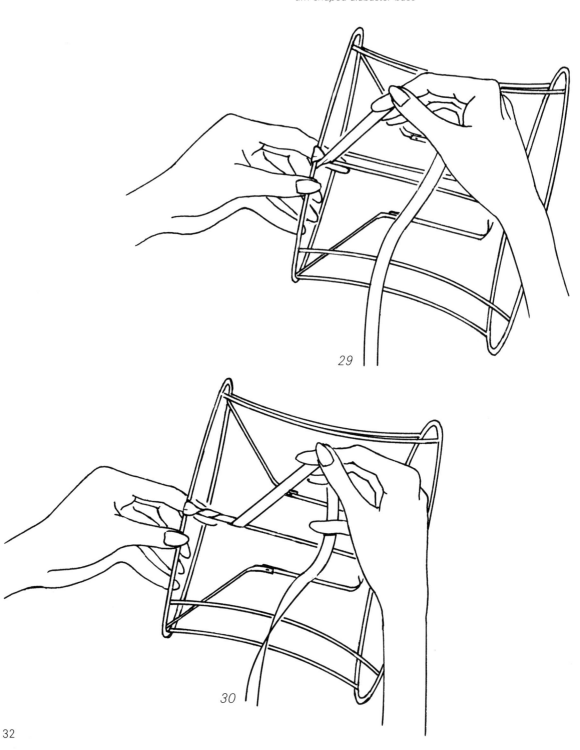

29

30

32 *Finishing off taping a strut round bottom ring*

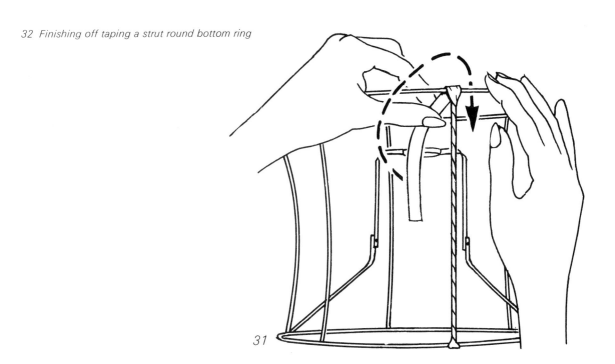

31

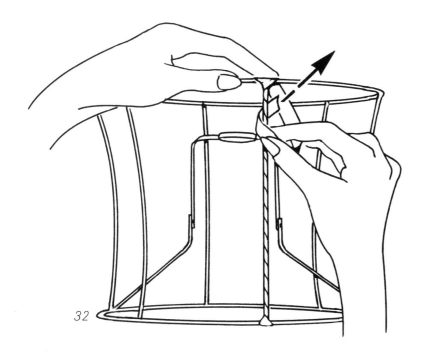

32

2 At the bottom of the strut turn the lampshade
   to the position in diagram 31. Wind the tape
   round the bottom ring, going first to the left
   and then to the right of the ring. This is a
   figure of eight. Finish off with a knot as in
   diagram 32 and pull tightly. The end of the
   tape should come from the front of the frame.
   Trim off end to bottom ring. It is not necessary to stitch the end. If it has been taped
   tightly it will not unwind.
3 Tape each strut in this way and then tape top
   and bottom rings, making a figure of eight
   round each strut (diagrams 33 and 34).

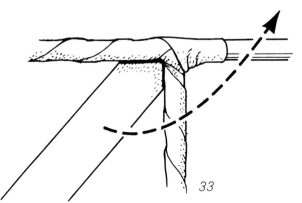

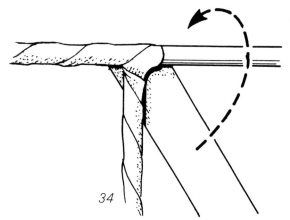

33, 34 Taping top and bottom rings, making a figure of
eight round each strut

9 Tailored shades with balloon lining

This method of making lampshades is the basic and most useful one, as once it has been mastered it is reasonably quick and easy. It can be used for most shades, ie straight-sided empire, curved empires, drums, ovals and some square-type shades.

The cover and lining are prepared in exactly the same way, using double material and pinning on to one half of the frame only. The cover is stitched to the frame first, and then the balloon lining is inserted.

Tailored shades made by this method should, if possible, have the material pinned to the frame with the selvedge or straight grain running from the top of the frame to the bottom (diagram 35). In this way the fabric is easier to work. Material that is stretched on the straight grain springs back to its original position more easily than material stretched on the cross. It is therefore easier to rectify errors in pinning and stretching.

It is, however, sometimes necessary to pin the material on to the frame on the cross grain, for example, when making a waisted lampshade (see diagram 13). Here, the top of the frame is larger in diameter than the middle, and the maximum amount of stretch is needed in order to get the cover, when stitched at the side seams, over the top of the frame.

Method
Bowed empire lampshade with a balloon lining

Materials:
25·4 cm (10 in.) bowed empire frame.
45·8 cm ($\frac{1}{2}$ yd) cover material
45·8 cm ($\frac{1}{2}$ yd) lining material
Approx. 7·3 m (8 yds) 1·3 cm ($\frac{1}{2}$ in.) lampshade tape.

Fitting fabric to frame
1 Tape the frame (see chapter 8).
2 Fold fabric in half with right sides together. Place on to one side of the frame only with fold at the top and place a pin in each corner to hold the fabric together. The material is placed on the frame on the straight grain with the selvedge running from the top to the bottom of the frame (diagram 35).
3 Place a pin at ABC and D pinning just into the top of the tape and not behind the back of the frame (diagram 35).
4 Pin fabric to the two side struts (AC and BD) placing pins at 2·5 cm (1 in.) intervals. Do not pin at top and bottom rings until most of the fullness has been taken to the

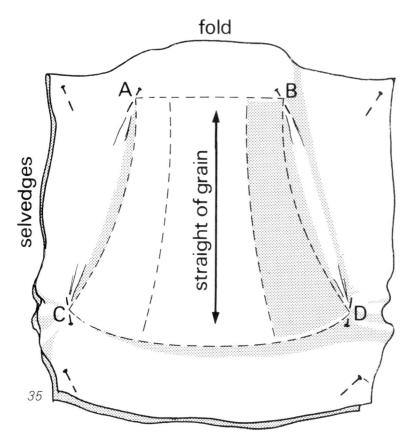

fold

selvedges

straight of grain

A B

C D

35

sides (diagram 36). (Always place pins on the side struts with the heads facing the centre of the shade. Pins on the top and bottom rings should face towards the centre. This reduces the risk of damaging clothes and body.)

5 Tighten fabric to top and bottom rings to remove wrinkles, pinning every 2·5 cm (1 in.).

6 Complete pinning on side struts, inserting pins first at 1·3 cm ($\frac{1}{2}$ in.) intervals and then finally at 0·6 cm ($\frac{1}{4}$ in.) intervals.

7 With a soft pencil carefully mark over the pins on the side struts, extending the line 1·3 cm ($\frac{1}{2}$ in.) above A and B and C and D and extending the pencil mark 1·3 cm ($\frac{1}{2}$ in.) round the top and bottom rings at ABC and D (diagram 36).

8 Leaving the corner pins in to hold the fabric together, take out all pins from the frame.

9 Machine down the pencil line from top to bottom, using a medium sized stitch and stretching fabric very slightly while machining. This avoids the stiches breaking when the cover is stretched over the top of the frame.

10 Trim seams to 0·6 cm ($\frac{1}{4}$ in.) at each side. Cut along fold line at top (diagram 37).

11 Prepare the lining in exactly the same way as the outer cover and then set aside.

Application of cover

1 Press the cover keeping the fabric flat – do not press the seam open.

2 Slip cover over the frame with the right side on the outside. Make sure that the seams

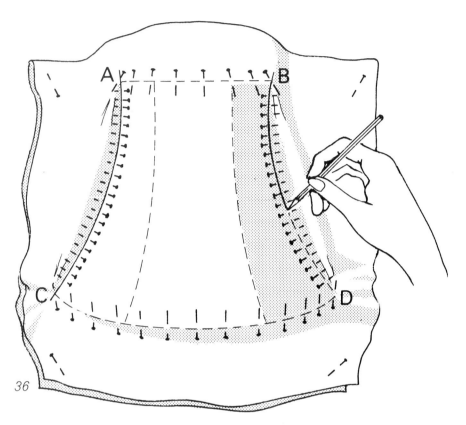

36

35 Placing material with selvedge running from top to
   bottom of frame: inserting first pins
36 Taking out fullness by pinning fabric to side struts first.
   Mark seamline with pencil

are placed on to the side struts with the
seams behind the strut.

3 Match horizontal pencil line at top and
  bottom rings.

4 Pin round top and bottom rings of lampshade gradually tightening the fabric. Place
  pins at 2·5 cm (1 in.) intervals (diagram 38).
  Here again it is important to make sure that
  the pins are placed so that they avoid unnecessary damage to clothes and body.

5 With a No. 9 sharps needle and a short
  length of double matching thread, oversew
  cover to frame. Do not use a long piece of
  thread or this will knot more easily and
  catch round the pins. The oversewing stitch
  should be on the outside edges of the top
  and bottom rings and the sewing should be
  from right to left (diagram 38).

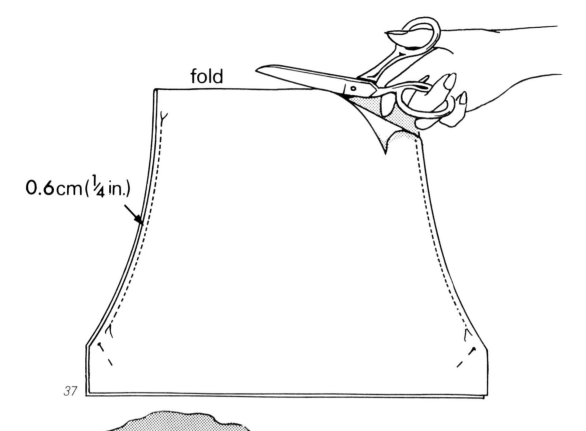

fold

0.6cm (¼ in.)

37

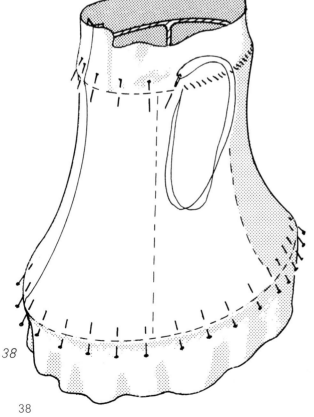

38

37 Cutting along fold line at top of fabric
38 Pinning fabric to lampshade at 2·5 cm (1 in.) intervals.
Oversewing: position and direction of stitches

6 Cut away surplus fabric from top and bottom of lampshade, trimming close up to the stitches. As these have been sewn with double thread they will not break away and should be quite firm. If this surplus material is not cut away very close to the stitching it will make a bulky finish when the lining is inserted (diagram 39).

Application of balloon lining

1 Press lining flat and do not press seams open. Drop lining into the shade matching seams and horizontal pencil marks at top and bottom rings.
2 Pin lining to top and bottom rings, making sure that the pins are placed on the outside

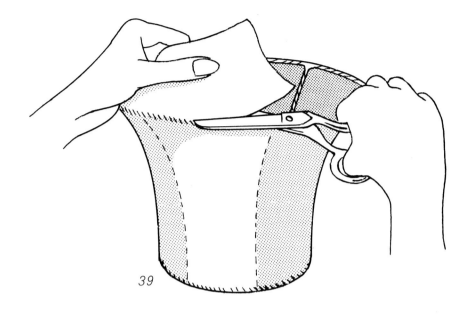

39

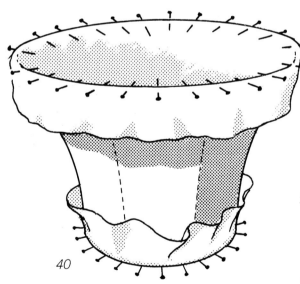

40

edge of the shade (diagram 40). Adjust lining by tightening pins at top and bottom of shade until the lining is taut and smooth and all fullness has been disposed of.

3 When pinning the lining round the top ring, unpick seam down to horizontal pencil mark and spread out material to enable the lining to sit neatly round the gimble fitting (diagram 41).

4 Stitch lining to frame with an oversewing stitch and double matching thread in the same way as the outer cover. The stitches should be on the outer edge of the lampshade so that they are covered completely when the trimming is applied.

39 Cutting away surplus after stitching is completed
40 Pinning lining to top and bottom rings

Opposite
Curved empire lampshade on a converted brass candlestick

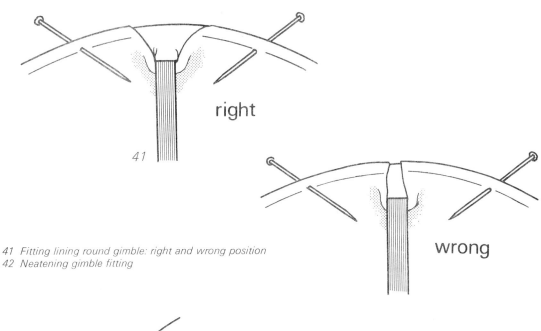

41 Fitting lining round gimble: right and wrong position
42 Neatening gimble fitting

right

wrong

41

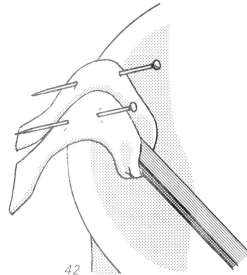

42

To neaten the gimble fitting

From a piece of lining fabric, cut a piece of crossway strip 10·2 cm (4 in.) long and 2·5 cm (1 in.) wide. Fold in three to make a strip 1·3 cm ($\frac{1}{2}$ in.) wide. Press. Slip under gimble fitting and pin in position as in diagram 42. Oversew securely in place on stitching line for lining, keeping stitches well down on to the outside of the shade.

10 Tiffany lampshades

Tiffany lampshades blend well with traditional and modern furnishing schemes and look effective in bathrooms, kitchens, bedrooms and dining rooms. They can be treated in a variety of ways.

Here are two methods of covering a tiffany-style lampshade. One is simple, fairly quick and easy to make; it consists of making a tube with a casing at the top and bottom through which elastic is threaded. A lining is not used and the cover can be removed for washing.

The other method is more tailored and takes longer to make as the fabric is sewn on to the frame in sections. An external lining is used as a balloon lining is not practicable on this shape of frame.

Tiffany-style frames vary considerably in shape, so buy one that is suitable for the method chosen (see diagrams 9, 10 and 11).

Method 1   Gathered tiffany with frill

This is suitable for light-weight fabrics only and those that have good draping qualities. Suitable fabrics are lace, voile, lawn, broiderie anglaise, and light dress cottons. Heavier fabrics are best made up using Method 2.

1 Paint the frame and tape the top and bottom rings. It is not necessary to tape the struts but they must be painted.
2 A rectangle of fabric is needed which should be the length of the circumference of the bottom ring, plus 10 cm (4 in.). The width should be the measurement of the strut, plus 7·6 cm (3 in.). If it is necessary to join the fabric to obtain the required length, cut two pieces of equal size.
3 Join the fabric with a french seam to make a tube. Press seam flat.
4 To make the casing at the top and bottom edge, turn over 1·3 cm ($\frac{1}{2}$ in.) and press, and then turn over another 1·3 cm (diagram 43). Press. Machine along top and bottom edges of casing leaving 1·3 cm open for inserting elastic (diagram 44).
5 Insert a narrow tape or piece of string into the casing at top and bottom and slip on to frame. Adjust tape to fit and mark to get the length of elastic required.
6 Mark position of frill with tailor's chalk or tacking cotton. This is the fitting line (diagram 45).
7 Take off shade and insert required length of elastic, sewing the ends firmly together.
8 To make the frill, cut a strip of fabric on the straight grain of the material (10 cm (4 in.) wide and 1$\frac{1}{2}$ times the circumference of the

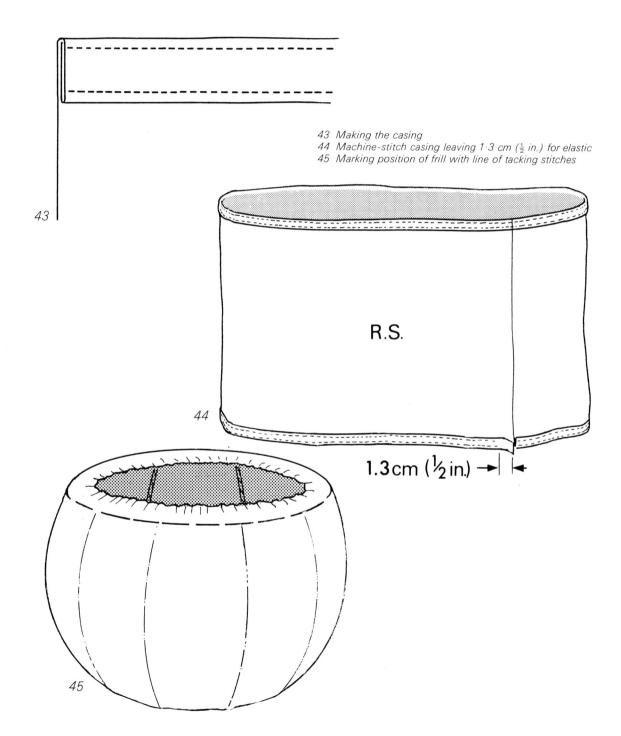

43 Making the casing
44 Machine-stitch casing leaving 1·3 cm ($\frac{1}{2}$ in.) for elastic
45 Marking position of frill with line of tacking stitches

43

R.S.

44

1.3cm ($\frac{1}{2}$ in.)

45

46

46 Running stitch for frill passes through two layers of fabric
47 Frill applied on fitting line

47

bottom ring. Join the ends of the strip together with a narrow french seam.
9 Fold in half lengthwise and turn in raw edges 1·3 cm at top edge. Run a row of running stitches along the fabric 1·3 cm from top (diagram 46). Gather up frill and adjust to fit the bottom of the lampshade.
10 Apply frill to cover of lampshade along the fitting line (diagram 47).

Method 2 Tailored tiffany lampshade

This method can be used for many fabrics, as the material is stretched on to the frame on the cross in four sections. A variety of effects can be achieved using this method. The seams are then covered with pieces of crossway strip. Suitable fabrics include lawn, broderie anglaise, silks, rayon dupion, light cottons and light furnishing fabrics. Plain or patterned fabric can be used. However, avoid using stripes, as these can prove difficult to match successfully. If using broderie anglaise for the outside cover, consider the possibility of having a brightly coloured lining – this is most attractive and shows up the embroidery well.

An external lining is used with a tailored shade and this is applied before the top cover, and in exactly the same way. A balloon lining

is not practicable because of the shape of the frame.

When making a tailored tiffany avoid using a frame that has a very marked convex curve at top and bottom (see diagram 9). These usually have more struts and are more successful made up in the gathered style (see page 42).

Materials

For a 25·4 cm (10 in.) frame 7·6 cm (3 in.) across the top and 22·9 cm (9 in.) deep)

91 cm (1 yd) of 91 cm (36 in.) wide cover fabric

91 cm (1 yd) 91 cm (36 in.) wide lining fabric

Approx. 11 m (12 yds) lampshade tape

91 cm (1 yd) fringe or braid for the trimming

1 Tape the frame (chapter 8).
2 Place the lining material over a quarter of the frame on the cross of the fabric (diagram 48).
3 Place pins at ABC and D to hold fabric to frame, making sure that the pins are placed with the points facing the middle of the section to avoid unnecessary scratching. Smooth fabric over the frame and pin to top and bottom rings along AB and CD and down the two struts AC and BD, easing out any fullness (diagram 48).

48, 49 Position of straight grain of fabric. Oversewing fabric to frame leaving 5 cm (2 in.) fabric at top and bottom for neatening edges
50 Trimming surplus fabric away close to stitching

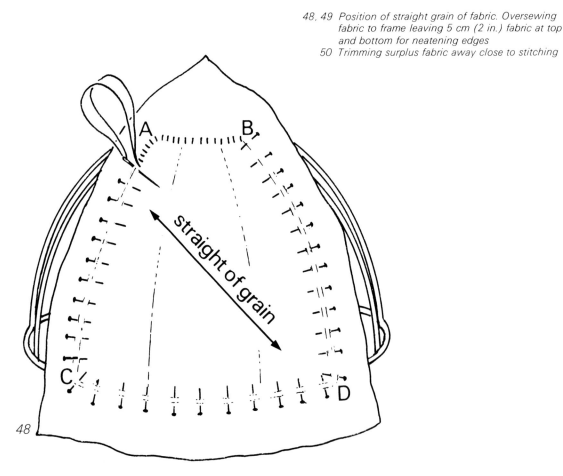

49

50

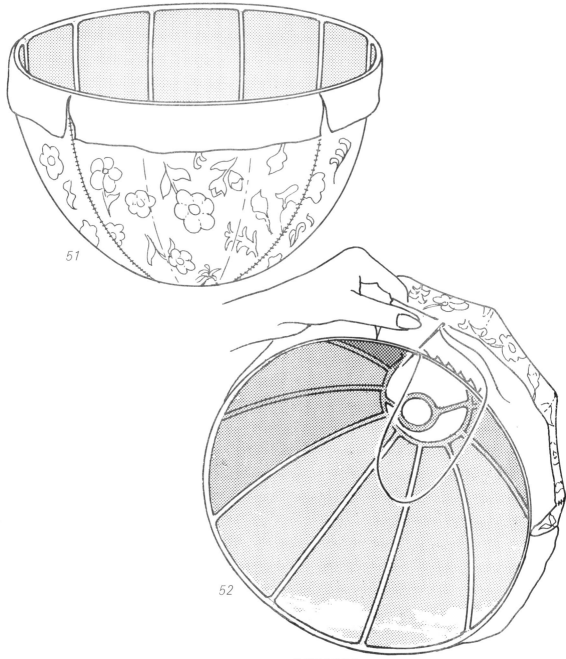

51

52

PLATES 2 AND 3
Curved empire shade on a converted brass candlestick
Square type shade on a converted Chinese vase

4 When all the fullness has been disposed of and the fabric is smooth and taut, oversew fabric to frame using matching thread. Working from right to left start sewing at B, continue along to A, then to C, D and back to B (diagram 48).

5 Trim away surplus fabric from the two struts AC and BD. At top and bottom rings AB and CD trim off to leave 5·1 cm (2 in.) of fabric for neatening the edges (diagram 49).

6 Apply the lining to the other three-quarters of the frame in the same way.

7 When the lining has been completed on the whole of the frame, apply the top cover in exactly the same way, using the same struts for stitching. All the stitching is done on the outer edge of the struts as the raw edges are neatened by covering with crossway strips.

8 Trim top and bottom rings of cover close to stitching (diagram 50).

9 To neaten top and bottom rings, fold back lining fabric over top cover and sew as in diagrams 51 and 52. Trim material close to stitching.

Neatening the struts

10 To cover the stitching on the struts, prepare enough crossway strip 2·5 cm (1 in.) wide to fit down the four struts and also round the top ring (for directions as to how to make crossway strip see page 73). Make sure the fabric is cut on the direct cross. Apply adhesive evenly to the strip and apply over the stitches on the four struts. Stretch the crossway strip slightly when applying it and press it gently with the fingers to make it firm.

Trimming

For the top ring, crossway strip is usually the best choice, as it moulds to the shape of the curve, unlike most commercially-made trimmings. Apply in the same way as on page 68. The bottom ring can be trimmed with a decorative fringe or braid, or can be finished with crossway strip in the same way as the top ring.

11 Standard lampshades and shades for large bases

When making shades for large lamps and for standard lamps the same instructions can be followed as for the tailored shade with a balloon lining (chapter 9). The material is stretched on to the frame using double material and pinned to one half only. One or two processes, however, require extra care, eg estimating the fabric required, and fitting the balloon lining round the duplex fitting of the frame.

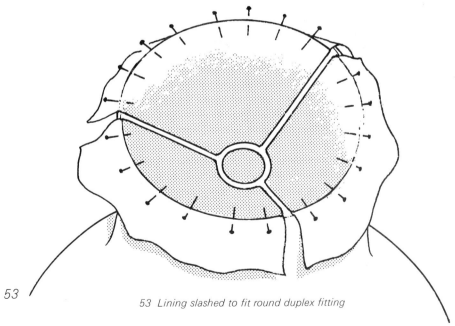

53

53 Lining slashed to fit round duplex fitting

Opposite
Tiffany lampshade in liberty lawn with a deep fringe

Estimating the amount of material

The easiest way of estimating the amount of fabric required is to measure the circumference of the shade and add an extra 10–15 cm (4–6 in.). Measure also the depth of the shade and add an extra 10–15 cm (4–6 in.). The amount of material needed for the lining is estimated in the same way. For example, a 61 cm (20 in.) frame which is 38 cm (15 in.) deep will need two widths of material as the circumference of the frame measures more than 91 cm (36 in.) (the normal width of dress fabrics, including crêpe-back satin). It will be found that most standard and larger frames require at least a yard of fabric for the outer cover and a yard for the lining, unless a wider furnishing fabric is being used.

Remember that it is easier to make a lampshade using the fabric on the straight grain (the selvedge running from the top to the bottom of the frame) and this applies particularly when working with larger shades. Fabric that is stretched on the cross grain does not spring back to its original shape as easily as when it is stretched on the straight grain. Therefore, mistakes cannot be so easily rectified in the pinning and stretching, if fabric is worked on the cross.

Fitting balloon lining

When fitting a balloon lining to a standard shade the same method is used as for the curved empire lampshade (chapter 9). However, with a large shade the fitting is usually a duplex one and not a gimbal one. This involves particular care when fitting the lining as it is necessary to slash the lining down where the duplex fitting is fixed to the top ring, in order to make the lining set well (diagram 53). If a deep enough cut is not made the lining will pucker, but if too deep a cut is made an ugly gap will be seen in the lining! Care and accuracy are necessary to achieve a good fit round each wire of the fitting. The fitting is then neatened with a crossway strip as on page 41).

12 Pleated and swathed lampshades

These shades are probably the most difficult to make successfully, and much patience and time is necessary to achieve a professional result. All the pleating must be evenly spaced to look effective.

Choose soft sheer fabrics that drape well, such as silk georgette or silk chiffon. Do not use nylon chiffon as this is too springy for pleating and does not drape satisfactorily. Rayon chiffon can be used and is slightly cheaper than the silk chiffon. Jap silk can be used with good effect for straight pleated drum shades, but is not suitable for swathed pleated shades.

When making a pleated or swathed lampshade it is advisable to apply the lining before beginning the pleating. This is to avoid any movement of the pleats once they are in position. A special lining is used, which is explained on page 54. This is an external lining which has the appearance of a balloon lining at the bottom ring. If a conventional balloon lining is applied in the usual way, after the top cover, it tends to disturb the pleats and makes them less taut, and often baggy.

Pleated drum lampshades
To estimate for fabric
The amount of fabric needed for a pleated drum shade is equal to the depth of the frame plus 5 cm (2 in.), and three times round the bottom ring.

1 Measure the circumference of the bottom ring and multiply by 3.
2 Measure the depth of the frame and add 5 cm (2 in.).

Thus, a 30 cm (12 in.) frame which is 25 cm (10 in.) deep and measures 89 cm (35 in.) round the circumference needs 91 cm (1 yd) of fabric:

Height 25 cm (10 in.), ie 25 cm (10 in)+5 cm (2 in.) = 30 cm (12 in.)

Circumference 90 cm (35 in.), ie 90×3 (35 in.×3) = 270 cm (105 in.)

Therefore, a total length of material 270 cm (105 in.) is required, measuring 30 cm (12 in.) deep. The fabric is usually 114 cm (45 in.) wide, so 114 cm (45 in.) into 270 cm (105 in.) means allowing three strips of fabric (see diagram 54). This is 91 cm (1 yd) of fabric.

The pleating should run down the selvedge grain of the fabric. This is important, as there is a definite grain to chiffon and georgette and the pleats will then set well if used in this way. Be sure, then, to plan the strips as in diagram 54 with the selvedge at each side. The same rule applies when planning a swathed pleated shade.

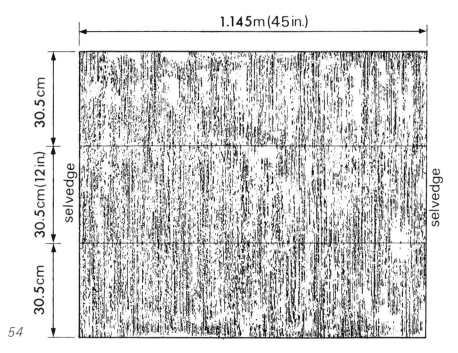

1.145m (45 in.)

30.5 cm

30.5 cm (12 in.)

selvedge

30.5 cm

selvedge

54

Method

1 Tape the frame in the usual way (chapter 8).
2 Prepare the lining as on page 35.
3 To apply the lining, place over top of lampshade on the outside of the struts and pin
   as in diagram 55. At each strut on the bottom
   ring, slash up to strut, slip lining under ring
   and pull up and over to the front edge of the
   bottom ring. This is done at each strut on
   the bottom ring and gives the appearance
   of a balloon lining. The lining at the top of
   the shade is simply pinned and sewn on to
   the outside of the top ring (diagram 55).
   No slashing down to the struts is necessary
   here.
4 Trim lining to stitching at bottom ring and
   at top ring trim off to leave 2·5 cm (1 in.).
   This is neatened later.
5 With a short length of double matching silk
   oversew lining to frame at top and bottom
   rings in the usual way (diagram 38).

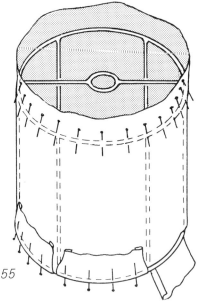

55

54 *Measuring up a piece of fabric for pleated shade*
55 *Pinning lining to frame: to outside of top ring, and*
   curled round inside of bottom ring, with slashes up to
   each strut and turn-ins 0·6 cm ($\frac{1}{4}$ in.) on each side edge

1.3 cm (½ in.) overlap of fabric at bottom ring

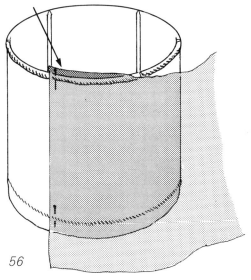

56

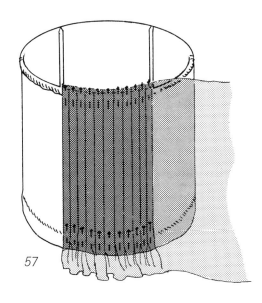

57

56 Placing material in position for pleating
57 One strut pleated and pinned ready for stitching
58 Neatening lining at top ring
59 Correct position for centre pleat

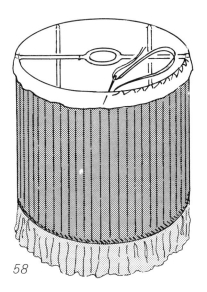

58

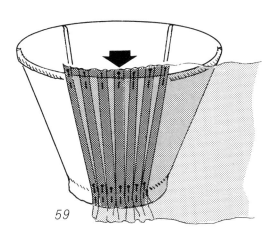

59

Pleating

6 Tear or cut the chiffon into strips 30 cm (12 in.) deep and cut off all selvedges. The strips of fabric are not seamed together, but are simply folded over each other during pleating.

7 Decide on the width of pleat required and whether an equal space is required between pleats. Pleats can vary in width from 0·6 to 1·3 cm ($\frac{1}{4}$–$\frac{1}{2}$ in.) depending on the fabric being used. Starting at the bottom ring turn in raw side edge of chiffon 0·6 cm ($\frac{1}{4}$ in.) (or the width of pleat), making sure that the fold is in line with the grain of the chiffon. Starting at a side strut and leaving 1·3 cm ($\frac{1}{2}$ in.) overlap at bottom ring (diagram 56) secure the chiffon with a pin at the bottom ring and at the top ring.

8 Leave a space the width of the pleat, and then make another pleat the same width as the first one.

9 Continue pleating in this way placing pins and pleating at the bottom ring only until the next strut is reached. It is most important that the overlap of 1·3 cm ($\frac{1}{2}$ in.) at the bottom ring (diagram 56) is kept in a perfectly straight line and that the fold lines are straight with the grain. This is the secret of successful pleating, and if this is not done, accurate pleating will not be achieved.

10 When the next strut is reached, start pulling up pleating to the top ring and pin each pleat into position. The pleats will fall into place and set well only if the fold lines of the pleats are straight with the grain.

11 When one section has been pinned in this way (diagram 57) oversew pleating round top and bottom rings using double thread in the usual way. Leave the first pleat pinned and do not stitch down. Make quite sure that each pleat has been pulled taut and is stitched securely.

12 Continue pleating round from strut to strut in this way, until the first strip of chiffon has been used.

13 To join the next strip of chiffon, overlap at the end of the first set of pleating to form a pleat. If possible, try to have this join on a strut. If it is necessary to trim away any surplus fabric, make sure a good clean line is cut with a sharp pair of scissors.

14 To finish off pleating, slip the end of the last pleat under the first pleat, which has not been stitched down (see stage 11 above). Finish stitching.

15 To neaten lining at top ring, trim chiffon back to stitching and fold lining over pleating (diagram 58) and neaten as in diagram 52. Trim off to stitching.

16 To neaten bottom edge turn back chiffon and neaten in the same way. Trim off to stitching.

17 Attach trimming as described in chapter 15, part (b).

60 *Line for measuring fabric required for swathed pleated lampshade*
61 *Pleating along the bottom ring showing 1·3 cm ($\frac{1}{2}$ in.) overlap*
62 *Missing one strut, to continue draping along top ring*

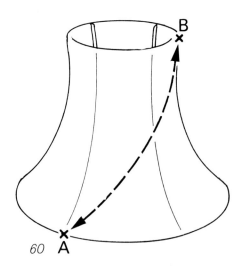

60 **A**

This is the simplest method of pleating when using pleats of 0·6–1·3 cm ($\frac{1}{4}$–$\frac{1}{2}$ in.) in length. It is, however, possible to measure and mark out the material with dots before commencing the pleating. This usually proves very tedious and does not necessarily achieve a better result than the method described here.

Swathed pleated lampshades

Swathed pleated lampshades are more difficult to make successfully than straight pleated ones, but with a little care and patience a good result can be achieved. Try making a straight pleated one first to gain practice with pleating.

A curved empire shaped frame is needed for this type of shade.

To estimate the amount of fabric required, allow three times the circumference of the bottom ring. To obtain the depth of the material needed, measure the lampshade with a tape measure from the bottom of the first strut A and up and across to the top ring B, missing out one strut (diagram 60). Add an extra 7·6 cm (3 in.) to this measurement.

Method

1 Tape the frame in the usual way (chapter 8).
2 Prepare and apply the lining as for the straight pleated drum lampshade (page 54).
3 Prepare chiffon by tearing or cutting it into strips of the required depth and cutting off the selvedges.
4 Pin the first pleat in position folding in the raw edge. Pleat and pin the material on to the bottom ring until one section of the frame has been completed (diagram 61). Leave an equal space between each pleat and keep the fold of the pleat in line with the grain of the fabric, and keep a 1·3 cm ($\frac{1}{2}$ in.) overlap along the bottom ring.
5 To drape the fabric to the top ring, take the first pleat and drape up and across to the top ring stretching the fabric gently. Miss the next strut and pin to the following one (diagram 62). Continue draping each pleat in turn. There must be the same number of pleats at the top ring as at the bottom ring, but as the same amount of material has to be fitted into the top section, the pleats at

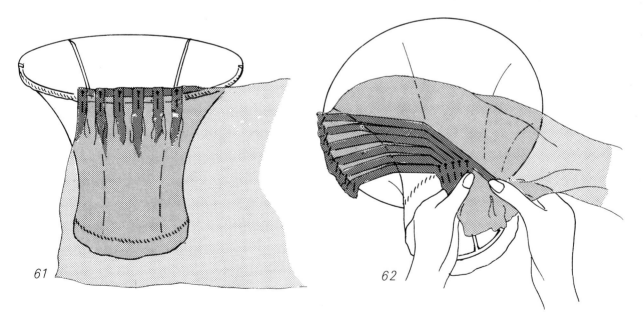

61

62

the top will be much smaller and will overlap considerably.

6 When one section has been completed satisfactorily, adjust pins at top and bottom rings to make sure pleats are taut and flat.

7 Oversew this section at the top and bottom ring leaving only the first pleat pinned, so that the last pleat can be tucked underneath at the end.

8 Continue pleating and draping each section in turn, checking that each has the same number of pleats.

9 At the last strut, trim off material and tuck under the first pleat. Finish stitching.

10 Neaten lining at top ring as in diagrams 52 and 58.

11 To neaten bottom edge turn back chiffon and neaten in the same way. Trim off to stitching.

12 Apply trimming (see chapter 15). Metallic laces and narrow velvet ribbons used together look particularly well on pleated and swathed lampshades. The laces should be sewn on in the usual way and the velvet ribbon applied with an adhesive. (See chapter 15, part (b).)

Pages 58 and 59
Pleated chiffon swathed

13 Sectional lampshades — working with difficult fabrics

This method of making lampshades can be used when an unusual frame is being used, for half and three-quarter shades and shields, or when using fabric that is difficult to work with, ie one that has little stretch or 'give'. It is a particularly useful way of making up materials that would normally be considered unsuitable for lampshade making, eg glazed chintz, and some furnishing fabrics, or velvets, because of their lack of elasticity. It is also a suitable method when embroidered panels and pieces of fabric with pronounced motifs are being used. It is also a good method when using pieces of fine sewing that need to be accurately centred on the frame.

Each panel or section is sewn separately on to the frame, or sometimes two to three panels can be covered together (as in the tiffany lampshade (see chapter 10). Either a balloon lining or an external lining can be used depending on the shape of the frame. If a 30 cm (12 in.) or larger square-shaped frame is being used it is advisable to apply the lining in sections in the same way as the outer cover, so that there is the minimum of movement of the lining.

Square sectional shade
Method
1 Tape the frame in the usual way (chapter 8).

2 The lining is applied to the frame before the top cover (see diagrams 48, 49 and 50).
3 For the top cover, the two larger sections are worked first and then the two smaller side ones. With the fabric on the cross, place the material over the front section of the frame. Pin at top and bottom of the frame using only a few pins to hold the fabric in position (diagram 63).
4 Insert three pins halfway down the section at both sides, pulling gently across the frame. Continue pinning down both sides and along top and bottom of the frame, pulling the fabric gently to mould to the shape of the frame.
5 After pinning all four sides work round the section removing each pin in turn, stretching the fabric so that it is firm and taut, and is without any wrinkles or creases.
6 When the panel has been satisfactorily pinned and stretched, oversew with double matching thread. Start sewing at the top right-hand corner A and work along the top of the frame to B, down the side strut, along the bottom ring CD and up to A (diagram 63). Remove each pin one at a time so that the material stays firmly stretched over the section.

7 Work the back section in the same way and then the two side sections.
8 Trim away surplus fabric at struts and top and bottom rings and finish as in diagrams 51 and 52.
9 Apply crossway strip down each corner strut and round the top and bottom of the lamp-shade. A more elaborate trimming could also be used at top and bottom if desired.

63 *Pinning a sectional lampshade with straight grain of fabric placed diagonally on frame*

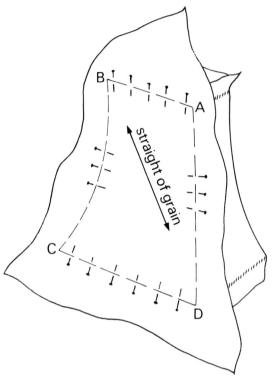

63

14 Candle shades and wall lights

These are made using the same methods given for full-size shades, but because they are so much smaller, they are often more fiddly to make. However, they are well worth the time and effort involved as they can be most costly to buy.

Shades for wall lights and chandelier type fittings usually have butterfly clip fittings, which enable the shade to clip onto the bulb. It is important that the bulb is kept as far away as possible from these small lampshades, and so balloon linings are seldom used. They would become scorched and discoloured in a short time. Use an external lining and low wattage bulbs with small shades to avoid the risk of scorching and discoloration.

Frames for wall lights and chandelier type fittings come in various basic shapes, but unusual designs can sometimes be found or could be made up to order.

Half shades and shields which are also very popular can be obtained in large stores, and are suitable for use where only the front of the shade is seen. Three-quarter shades would be the best choice for situations where the shade is also viewed from the side. These cover more of the bulb than a half shade.

The light from half and three-quarter shades is reflected against the wall and back into the room, and so these tend to give more light than a full shade. They are not, of course, suitable for chandelier or candelabra-type fittings, as they do not hide the bulb completely.

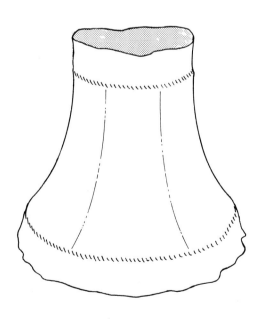

64 Applying lining before cover on a small shade

63

Method

When making complete shades for wall lights or candelabra-type fittings, follow the directions for the outer cover as on page 35. The lining is prepared in the same way, but is applied to the frame *before* the top cover and stitched on to the frame as in diagram 64. The top cover is then slipped on top of the lining and stitched in the usual way. The top and bottom rings are neatened as in diagrams 51 and 52.

When making half and three-quarter shades follow the directions for making sectional shades (see chapter 13), trimming off fabric all round the shade. The trimming on these shades should be applied all round the frame in order to cover the stitching (diagram 65).

65 *Trimming applied to all edges of half-shade*

15 Trimmings

(a) Choice of trimmings

A good choice of trimming which complements the texture of the fabric and design of the frame can give a lampshade a professional look.

A trimming has two functions — it can be purely decorative, but it is frequently used to cover stitching and seams. Too often, however, a lampshade can be spoilt by the wrong choice of decoration. A trimming should complement the lampshade fabric, not detract from its simplicity. Beware of using fussy trimmings, which usually do not enhance a lampshade, but merely make it look home-made. Consider the plainer and more tailored braids and trimmings which give a more professional finish. These are often less costly than the more elaborate trimmings, but look far more elegant. A tailored lampshade looks well with a plain trimming, but remember also that a pleated chiffon shade might also benefit from a plain trim rather than one that is too fussy.

There are many attractive commercially made trimmings from which to choose — there are also some badly made ones! They can be found in all widths and textures and some can even be dyed to match individual colour schemes.

Fashions in trimmings change, so be on the look out for new ideas and be aware of current trends. Take the trouble to look at expensive couture shades to see what is being used, and make a note of interesting ideas.

When choosing a trimming for a lampshade, remember to take into consideration the texture and colour of the outer fabric as well as the base for which it is being made. For example, if the lampshade is of a traditional design made of fine silk, then a silk trimming would be suitable. If, on the other hand, the lampshade is made of hessian or some other coarsely woven fabric and is for a pottery base, then a cotton braid or one with a matt finish would probably be more appropriate. Always relate the trimming to the base and to the fabric as well as to the colour. If an exact colour match cannot be found, try using a contrasting colour or one that is used in some other item of soft furnishing in the room, providing the colours work well together.

Types of trimmings

1 Lampshade braid: this is a loosely woven braid found in many colours and patterns, and usually made from cotton or rayon, and sometimes silk. It is specially designed for use with lampshades and should not be confused with upholstery gimp; this is less flexible and more closely woven than lampshade braid, and is not therefore as suitable for trimming

shades as it does not mould easily to a curve.

2 Rayon/Silk bobble fringe: mostly made from silk or rayon and interspersed with small wooden balls covered in silk. This fringe is rather costly.

3 Cotton bobble fringe: similar to the above but much less costly as the bobbles are made from compressed cotton. White bobble fringe can be dyed quite easily at home if a suitable colour cannot be obtained.

4 Tassel fringe: usually made from silk or rayon. The fringe is made in various depths and is interspersed with tassels of various sizes.

5 Fringing: a plain fringe made from rayon or cotton in many depths and thicknesses. Can be a cut fringe or a looped fringe.

6 Russia braid: an artifical silk cord which can be used very successfully combined with a hand-made crossway strip. Particularly attractive in a *Lurex* finish.

7 *Lurex* braids and laces: there are many attractive metallic braids and laces available which, when carefully chosen, can be most effective. Most of these wash well.

8 Velvet ribbon: this is a most useful form of trimming as it looks well on either delicate lampshades or on coarse ones, such as those covered in hessian. However, as it will not stretch easily and mould to a curve, it is not suitable for all types of shades, particularly those with well-defined curves. It is particularly suitable, though, for drum shapes, and can be used in conjunction with other trimmings. Velvet ribbon also looks well on pleated and swathed shades. Use narrow width ribbon: the wider widths can be used successfully on drum shapes. It can also be gathered up to make a more elaborate trimming (see part (c), page 68, on handmade trimmings).

9 Other types of trimmings can be used for decorating lampshades, including piping cord, appliquéd motifs, dried flowers or leaves, etc. These are also described in the chapters on firm lampshades (pages 78 to 86) as they are more appropriate for that type of shade.

(b) Application of trimmings

As a rule the trimming should always be sewn on to the shade unless a better, more even effect can be achieved by using an adhesive, with for example velvet ribbons and crossway strip. This might also apply to russia braid and narrow trimmings that are too awkward to sew on successfully.

Always measure very accurately for the amount of trimming required, and allow an extra few inches on top of that measurement. Trimmings are usually eased on and this takes up more length than might be thought. It is preferable to have a few centimetres or inches over than be just a little short.

Method

1 *Braids, bobble fringes, fringing and tassel fringe*

To sew on the trimming, cut the end straight and fold in 1·3 cm ($\frac{1}{2}$ in.). Starting at a side strut, pin on trimming and sew as in diagrams 66(*a*) and (*b*), using a zigzag type stitch, taking a stitch at the top and bottom of the trimming alternately. Take care that the stitching does not go through to the inside of the shade. Butt the two ends together (diagram 66(*c*)) and slip-stitch together. The trimming should be eased on to the shade and not stretched. When sewing on a bobble fringe or any type of fringing, beware of sewing on the trimming too tightly. This will pull the trimming to the inside of the bottom ring and the fringing will not hang well.

2 *Velvet ribbons*

As these have very little elasticity they need to be stretched on to the shade and fixed with an adhesive (eg *Uhu*). Butt the ends in the same way as in Method 1 but do not slip stitch together. By sticking rather than sewing this trimming on to the shade, a more even finish is achieved.

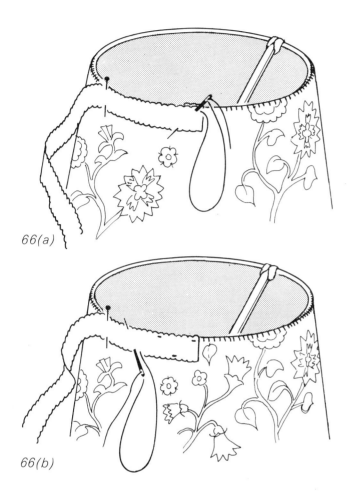

66(a)

66(b)

66(a) and (b) Long stitch hidden between braid and
cover of lampshade

66(c)

66(c) Ends of braid butted together

3 *Crossway strip*

Follow the instructions for making this on page 73.

(i) Prepare enough crossway to fit round the top and bottom of the shade.

(ii) When attaching to top and bottom of lampshade, apply end of strip to outside edge of lampshade, starting 0·6 cm ($\frac{1}{4}$ in.) beyond a side strut (diagram 67). Apply the adhesive to the strip using a small knife to spread it evenly. Great care is needed when doing this as the adhesive can easily mark the fabric. If too much is used on a thin fabric, the adhesive will soak through and mark the outside of the crossway strip.

(iii) Apply the strip a few inches at a time and press gently to the shade to achieve a perfectly even finish. The strip should just cover the oversewing stitches, but should not extend to the inside of the shade.

(iv) To finish off, turn in 0·6 cm ($\frac{1}{4}$ in.) at the end of the strip, secure with a little adhesive and apply over the other end (diagram 67).

When applying the strip to top and bottom

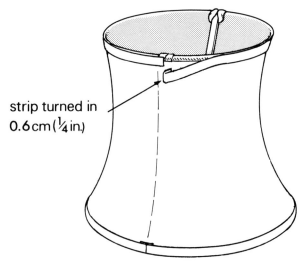

strip turned in
0.6 cm ($\frac{1}{4}$ in.)

67 *Placing two joins on same side of lampshade*

of a lampshade, make sure that the two joins are on the same side of the shade.

This trimming can also be used very successfully to cover seams on tiffany and sectional shades and is less conspicuous than commercially-made braids.

(c) Hand-made trimmings

Handmade trimmings can look well on certain lampshades, but great care should be taken to be sure that they are beautifully made and do not give an amateurish look to the lampshade. The same careful thought is necessary when choosing these as when choosing commercially made trimmings. They should be similar in weight and texture to the outer cover of the shade and must be dense enough to cover the stitching. Most of these trimmings are probably more successful used on soft shades than on firm shades.

1 *Tatting, crochet, lace, embroidery, macramé*

These can all be used for trimming lampshades. Remember to use a suitable thickness of thread. Decorative trimmings can also be made with automatic sewing machines with built-in embroidery stitches. Great care is needed when using these trimmings because they can make the lampshade look 'homemade' and unprofessional. If used skilfully, however, they can be very effective.

2 *Gathered velvet ribbon*

Use twice the circumference of the shade and make one or two rows of running stitches, depending on the width of the ribbon. Gather up and attach to the shade with adhesive. This gives a more satisfactory finish than stitching (diagram 68).

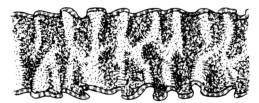

68 *Gathered velvet ribbon*

3 *Plaiting*

   (a) Russia braid looks well plaited (diagram 69). This can be obtained in a *Lurex* finish as well as in many colours.

   (b) Wool of various thicknesses can be used as a plait very successfully on firm lampshades.

   (c) Rushes can be plaited and look most effective used on firm lampshades, as the texture is most suitable for use with this type.

4 *Petal edged ruching*

Cut a strip of fabric 2·5 cm–3·8 cm (1–1½ in.) wide on the straight grain of the material. Turn in 0·6 cm (¼ in.) on both edges and press. Measure and mark 2·5 cm (1 in.) points along the fabric as in diagram 70. Work diagonal rows of small running stitches on the right side of the material (diagram 71). Draw up work (diagram 72) and apply to lampshade with adhesive, which is more satisfactory than stitching.

5 *Scalloped edge*

A scalloped edge made from the cover material can be made using an iron-on interfacing. This is particularly pretty when used on a tiffany style lampshade (see page 42).

1 Cut a strip of fabric 20–25 cm (8–10 in.) wide on the cross of the fabric, the length being the circumference of the bottom of the shade, plus 2·5 cm (1 in.) (ie 1·3 cm (½ in.) turnings) (diagram 73).

2 Join the ends of strip with 1·3 (½ in.) turnings, to make a circle, making sure the join is made on the straight grain. Press seam open.

3 With right sides together, fold in half and tack together (diagram 74).

69

70

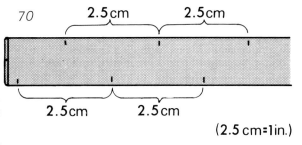

2.5cm   **2.5cm**

2.5cm   **2.5cm**

(2.5 cm=1in.)

71

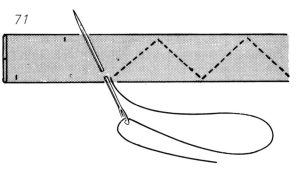

72

69 *Plaited Russia braid*
70 *Marking points for ruching 2·5 cm (1 in.) apart*
71 *Running stitches through points on ribbon*
72 *Finished effect of gathered stitches making petal edged ruching*

4 Make a paper pattern of each scallop to fit between the struts on the lampshade and place on fabric with the scalloped edge 1·3 cm ($\frac{1}{2}$ in.) from the fold (diagram 75).

5 Cut a piece of iron-on interfacing the exact size of the pattern and iron on to the fabric (diagram 75).

6 Mark round scallops accurately with tailor's chalk, and machine round line allowing 0·6 cm ($\frac{1}{4}$ in.) turnings (diagram 75).

7 Clip curves and cut away excess fabric

(diagram 76). Take out tacking and turn right sides out. Press.

8 With right sides together apply to bottom of lampshade using matching double thread. Oversew to base of shade allowing 0·6–1·3 cm ($\frac{1}{4}$–$\frac{1}{2}$ in.) turning (diagram 77). Trim off raw edge and turn band over to right side.

9 A narrow trimming or crossway strip could be fixed over the seam if desired (diagram 78).

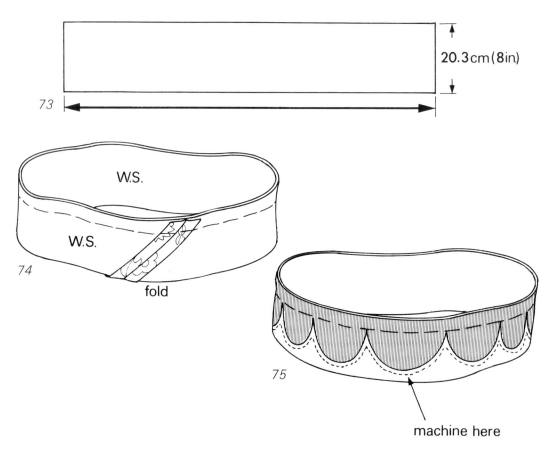

20.3 cm (8 in.)

73

W.S.

W.S.

74

fold

75

machine here

73 Circumference of bottom of lampshade plus 2·5 cm (1 in.) for turnings
74 Join made through straight grain of material
75 Iron-on interfacing applied, and scallops stitched

Opposite
Scalloped

76 *Cutting away surplus fabric, clipping into curves*
77 *Applying scalloped edge to lampshade*
78 *Finished effect*

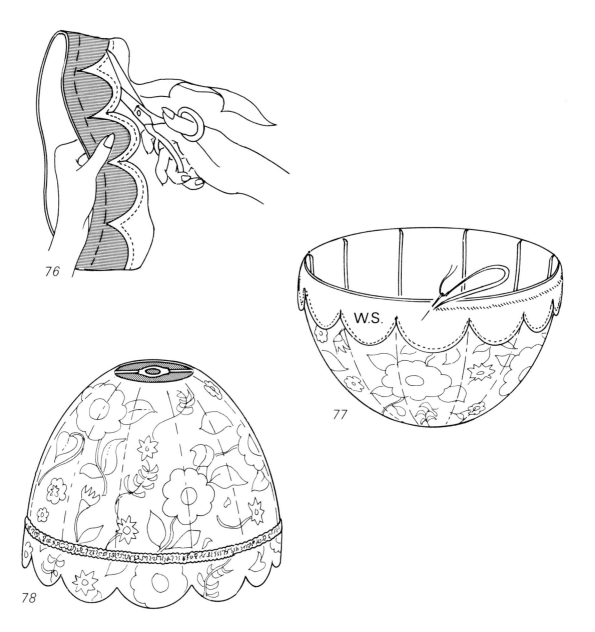

76

W.S.

77

78

(d) Crossway strip

This is one of the most useful types of trimmings. It can be made from odd pieces of fabric and is therefore most economical. It is easy to make and when well done, gives a most professional look to a lampshade. It can be used to cover stitches and seams and can also be used most effectively with other trimmings, such as metallic laces and braids.

To cut fabric on the cross

1 Fold the material diagonally so that the selvedge thread lies across the crossways thread, ie the warp across the weft (diagram 79). Press.
2 Cut along the fold. The material is then on the true bias and is rather like elastic; it will stretch to fit a corner or curve, but if stretched will not spring back to its original size.

3 In order to make all the strips the same size, make a ruler in stiff card 2·5 cm (1 in.) wide to use as a guide. 2·5 cm (1 in.) wide strips are the most suitable for trimming lampshades.
4 Place the edge of the ruler to the cut edge of the fabric and mark with a sharp piece of tailor's chalk. Cut along the line (diagram 80). Continue in this way until sufficient strips have been formed.
5 Fold the lengths in three and press, to make a crossway strip 1·3 cm ($\frac{1}{2}$ in.) wide (diagram 80a).
6 If joining the strips together to make one long strip, always make the join on the straight grain of the fabric (diagram 81). Place the right sides together and stitch the seam with a small stitch, making sure the strips form a 'V' as shown in diagram 82. Press the seam open.

79 To make crossway strip: folding fabric

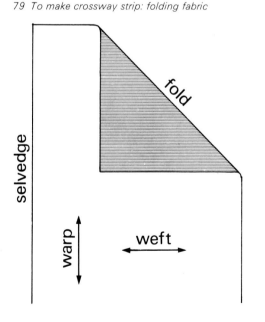

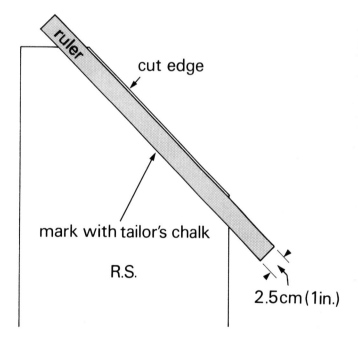

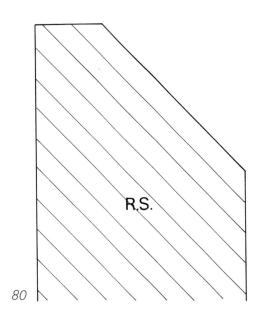

80(a)

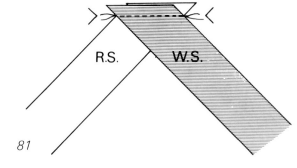

80

81

80 Cutting along fold line
80a Folding strip in three, then ironing flat
81 Joining crossway strip on straight grain
82 Final join: seam pressed open
83 Folding fabric to find direct cross

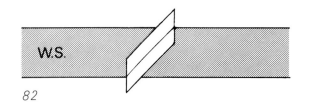

82

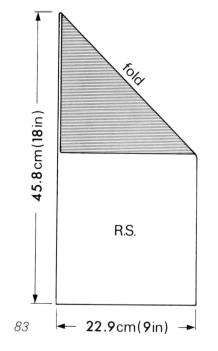

83

(e) Quick method of cutting on the cross

If large amounts of crossway strip are required, it is useful to be able to make it without having to join each strip individually. Many hours of work cutting and joining the strips can be saved if these simple instructions are followed. This method can also be used successfully in dressmaking and soft furnishing.

Method

23 cm ($\frac{1}{4}$ yd) 91 cm (36 in.) material makes 6·4 m (7 yd) of crossway strip 2·5 cm (1 in.) wide.

1 Take a strip of fabric 23 cm (9 in.) wide. The length of the strip should be at least twice the width, ie 46 cm (18 in.).
2 Fold over the top right-hand corner to obtain the direct cross (diagram 83).
3 Cut off this corner and join to lower edge with 0·6 cm ($\frac{1}{4}$ in.) seam (diagram 84). Machine this seam and press open (diagram 85). By adding this piece on to the bottom no material is wasted.
4 With a ruler 2·5 cm (1 in.) wide, mark lines on the right side of the fabric with a sharp piece of tailor's chalk, parallel to the top edge. Mark also 0·6 cm ($\frac{1}{4}$ in.) seam allowance down each side, and points A and B as shown in diagram 86.
5 Take a pin through the wrong side of the fabric at point A and take up to point B, pinning very accurately, with right sides together. Continue pinning along the seam. Tack and machine seam, checking first that the lines are matching. Press seam open, using a sleeve board (diagram 87).
6 Turn to right side and start cutting round the cylinder at the projecting strip at the top (diagram 88).

If plenty of fabric is available and no economy is necessary, the top right-hand corner and the bottom left-hand corner can be cut off and thrown' aside. This produces the same shaped piece of fabric, and has the advantage of producing fewer joins in the strip (diagram 89).

Square pieces of fabric can also be utilized in a similar way if cut and joined as in diagrams 90 and 91, placing AB to CD with right sides together.

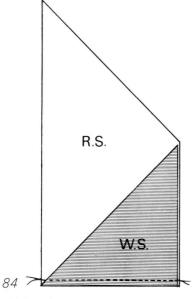

84 Cut off and join to lower corner
85 Machine stitch, press open

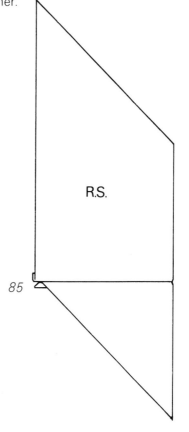

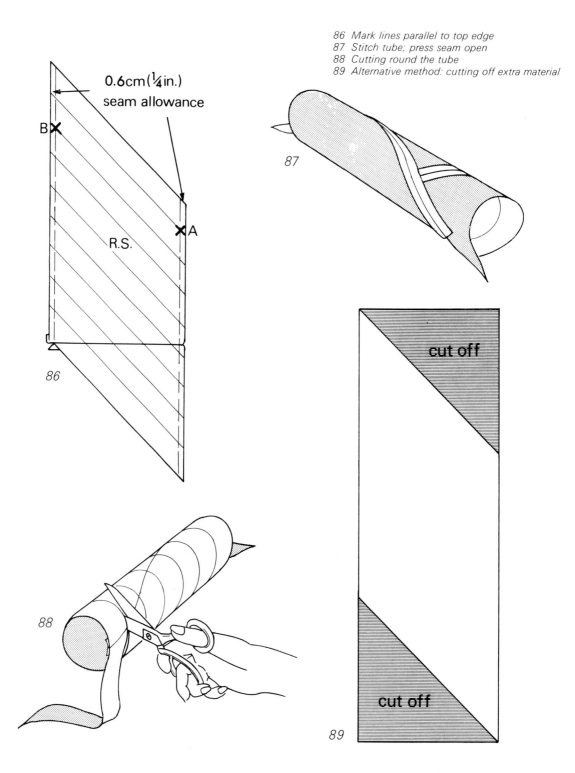

0.6cm (¼ in.) seam allowance

B✗

✗A

R.S.

86

86 Mark lines parallel to top edge
87 Stitch tube; press seam open
88 Cutting round the tube
89 Alternative method: cutting off extra material

87

cut off

88

cut off

89

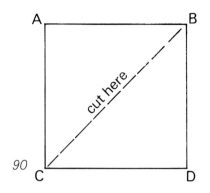
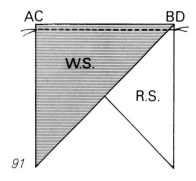

90 Making crossway strip using square piece of fabric
91 Machine stitch along new line AC–BD

Firm Lampshades

16 Choice of fabrics

Rigid or firm shades are quick and easy to make and very attractive shades can be made with a little imagination and the minimum of effort.

When choosing fabric for firm shades, remember that generally the plainer they are the more effective they look. Beware of making them fussy; keep the trimmings simple and match them in weight and texture to the fabric of the shade. This is not always easy, as the commercially made trimmings used for soft shades are very often quite unsuitable for firm shades. If using hessian for the cover fabric, for example, choose something suitable to match its rough texture. Plaited rushes, coarse wool or cotton trimmings could be used. Thick piping cord can be used effectively on some firm shades, and can be dyed to match the cover fabric if necessary.

Suitable materials

There are many materials available on the market for making firm shades and new ones are always being introduced. Be aware of current trends and experiment with new products. These are some that make very successful lampshades:

1 *Buckram:* a stiff cloth with a coarse rough weave which gives an interesting texture. It comes only in white, but can be tinted or dyed with oils or water colours and is a most useful foundation for a firm shade. It can be used for mounting more delicate fabrics, such as lace, organdie and gingham. It can also be used for appliqué decoration, using felt, cording, favourite pictures (footballers, cars, etc) and anything else that is interesting and decorative. With a little imagination most exciting results can be achieved. Dried flowers and leaves can also be mounted on to buckram and look most effective (diagram 92).

To use the buckram, wipe over the smooth side with a damp sponge before ironing on the fabric with a hot iron. Cover the fabric with a damp cloth and press again. Motifs of *guipure* lace, or pieces of embroidery can be fixed to the buckram using this method. If necessary, a small amount of adhesive (eg *Uhu*) could be used.

2 *Pelmet buckram:* this can also be used successfully. This buckram is impregnated with glue, is golden brown in colour (a good colour for lampshades) and has an interesting texture.

3 *Covered lampshade card:* this can be bought at most department stores and good handi-

craft shops and is ready to use. The range of colours and materials used on the card is fairly limited as are the widths available. However, fresh ones are being introduced all the time, so be on the look-out for new fabrics and designs. This ready-covered card is relatively expensive as it often involves a certain amount of wastage because of the set widths available.

4 *Parbond (iron-on lampshade parchment):* this is a lampshade parchment with an adhesive on one side. Light to medium weight fabrics can be applied to this. The material is placed on to the shiny side which is the adhesive side, and ironed on to the parchment with a hot iron. The heat releases the adhesive and the material sticks firmly to the surface. This is one of the most useful materials for making firm lampshades. Odd pieces of furnishing fabrics and dress fabrics can be used up in this way. If using delicate fabrics it is advisable to test a small piece first to make sure it will withstand a hot iron. If not, place a piece of heavier fabric or paper over the cover material before ironing on to the *Parbond*.

5 *Selapar:* this is a fairly new self-adhesive backing obtainable in board or *PVC*. It can be used with any kind of fabric except open-weave ones. The open part of the fabric catches the dirt and dust which then sticks to the *Selapar*.

To use *Selapar*, cut to the size required and gently peel off the protective paper and press the fabric to the sticky surface.

6 *Parchment:* Real parchment in the form of old maps, prints and deeds, can also be used for making firm lampshades, provided they are not stained and wrinkled.

ARSENAL

92 Mounting designs on to buckram for firm shades

17 Straight-sided drum lampshade

A straight-sided drum shade is the simplest of firm shades to make. Two rings are used for this shape and they must be exactly the same size; one should be plain and the other should have a fitting, eg gimble, duplex, etc. (see page 23).

Materials

2 25 cm (10 in.) rings (1 plain, 1 with fitting)
Approx. 5·5 m (6 yds) lampshade tape
0·9 m (1 yd) ready-prepared lampshade card
1·8 m (2 yds) trimming
12 wooden clothes pegs with springs
Uhu or similar adhesive
Needles (Betweens 5/6)

Method

1 Prepare the rings and tape in the usual way. When starting to tape the plain ring, however, it is advisable to secure the end of the tape to the ring with a little *Sellotape* (sticky tape) in order to avoid it slipping. Finish off the tape with a few oversewing stitches on the outside of the ring to keep the tape firmly in position. (These stitches will be covered by the lampshade card and will not show. Diagram 27.)

2 Measure round the taped rings to find the circumference of the shade, and decide on the height required.

3 Make a pattern using brown paper or card to try on to the rings. Allow 2·5 cm (1 in.) for the overlap. This will later be trimmed down to 0·6–1.3 cm ($\frac{1}{4}-\frac{1}{2}$ in.) seam allowance at the join.

4 Fit the paper pattern on to the taped rings using wooden clothes pegs. Check the proportion of the shade and the fit of the pattern. Make any adjustments that are necessary.

5 Cut out fabric very carefully, using paper pattern. Attach to the two rings using the wooden clothes pegs (diagram 93).

6 With double thread and a strong needle (Betweens 5/6), sew through the fabric to the tape round the top and bottom rings, using a blanket stitch (diagram 94). These stitches are covered by the trimming and therefore will not show on the outside of the lampshade. Take care that the lampshade fabric does not extend above the ring or it will give an ugly appearance (diagram 95).

7 Finish sewing 5 cm (2 in.) from where the seam will be positioned. Check the seam allowance and trim away to give 0·6–1·3 cm ($\frac{1}{4}-\frac{1}{2}$ in.) overlap depending on the fabric being used. A lighter fabric will require a smaller overlap than a heavier one.

Use a ruler and pencil to ensure a straight even edge, and make sure that the edge is cut with a sharp pair of scissors.

8 Overlap the seam and apply *Uhu* very carefully and evenly to both edges. Press together firmly with the fingers and hold until the seam is secure.

9 Finish blanket stitching at join at top and bottom rings.

Application of trimming

10 Sewing on a trimming to a hard rigid fabric would be impractical, so it is therefore applied with *Uhu*, or similar adhesive, which is spread evenly and thinly on to the trimming and then pressed firmly on to the shade until secure. The ends of the trimming should be turned in 0·6 cm ($\frac{1}{4}$ in.) and butted together. Any pattern should be matched if possible.

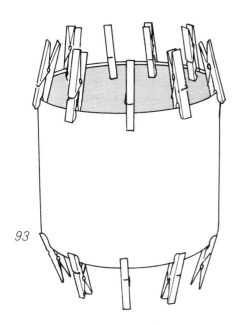

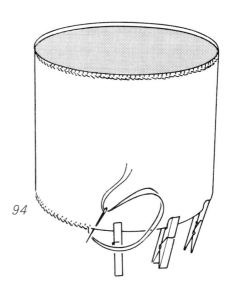

93 Position firm material with clothes pegs
94 Sew in place with blanket stitch
95 Position of taped ring: extending very slightly above the fabric

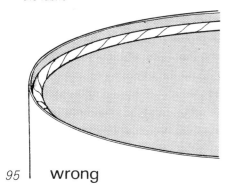

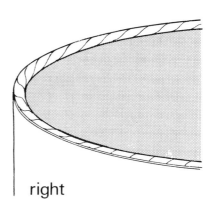

95   **wrong**   **right**

18 Near drums and oval shades

When making a cone shade, or a near-drum shade, that is to say a shade that is smaller at the top than at the bottom, it is necessary to make a pattern.

If possible, buy a frame which has struts. (If two rings have to be used, follow the directions in chapter 19.)

Method for taking a pattern
1 Tape the frame in the usual way.
2 Take a large piece of stiff brown paper or card. Place the taped lampshade frame on to the paper and hold it firmly.
3 Starting at the side strut, draw along the outside of the strut with a pencil and mark top and bottom. Rotate the frame slowly pen-

96 Taking a pattern

1.3 cm (½ in.) seam allowance

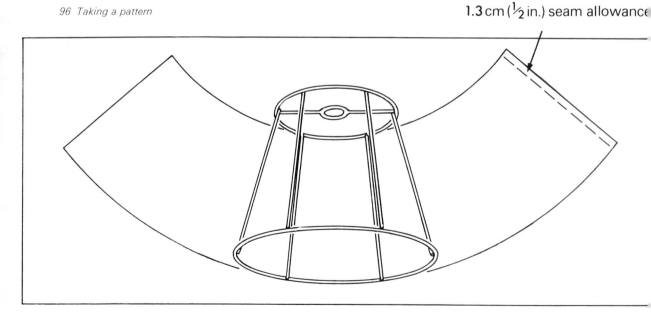

cilling along the top and bottom rings until the first strut is reached. Allow 1·3 cm ($\frac{1}{2}$ in.) seam allowance at one end (diagram 96). Take care not to let the lampshade frame slip, or an accurate pattern will not be obtained.

If a large frame is being used the pattern can be taken from one half of the frame only, and the lampshade made with two pieces cut from the same pattern. In this case, remember to reverse the pattern on the fabric for the second half (diagram 97).

4 Cut out the pattern and try on to the frame, adjusting where necessary.

5 It is important to fit the pattern correctly and adjust it, before cutting into the lampshade fabric.

6 Cut out the fabric from the paper pattern and peg on to the frame.

7 Proceed as for the straight-sided drum lampshade (see page 80).

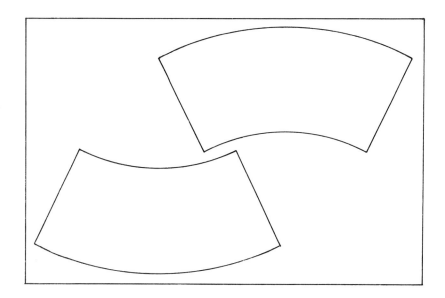

97 Cutting layout for cone lampshade covering material

19 Cone lampshades

When a strutted frame is not available in the size or shape required, a cone lampshade can be made using the two-ring method. For a first attempt at making a pattern, choose a small shade or one where the top ring is much smaller than the bottom ring.

In order to cut out the lampshade fabric accurately, it is necessary to make a paper pattern using graph paper. The measurements must be taken accurately and the pattern prepared carefully. The measurements should be taken over the taped rings otherwise the pattern will not fit the frame.

Making a pattern
Materials
Large sheet of graph paper
Sharp pencil
A long ruler
Set square or protractor
Pair of blackboard compasses — or use a strip of card or buckram with a hole for a pencil at one end and pivoting on a drawing pin at the other (diagram 100)

Method
1 Tape the rings in the usual way (chapter 8).
2 Take the measurements: (diagram 98)

(a) The height required for the shade.
(b) The diameter of the top ring (AB) and the circumference.
(c) The diameter of the bottom ring (CD) and the circumference.
3 On the graph paper draw a horizontal line CD which is the diameter of the bottom ring (diagram 99).
4 At the middle of CD, which is X, draw a vertical line from X to Y. This equals the required height of the shade. Angle YXD is a right angle of 90 degrees.
5 Draw a horizontal line through Y making it parallel with CD. AB equals the diameter of the top ring, with AY equal to YB.
6 Join CA and DB and continue these lines until they meet the perpendicular line at Z. If the pattern is accurate the two lines meet at the same point.
7 With a large compass and with Z as the centre, draw two arcs of circles; the first with radius ZB and the second with radius ZD. If a compass is not available, use a piece of buckram with a drawing pin in one end at Z. Make a hole in the buckram at the correct point and push a pencil point through it (diagram 100).
8 First draw the arc from point B round to

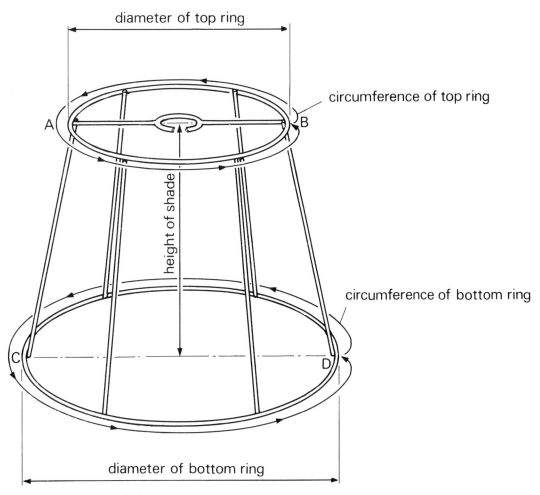

diameter of top ring

circumference of top ring

A

B

height of shade

circumference of bottom ring

C

D

diameter of bottom ring

98 Taking measurements required for cone lampshade pattern

point E (this is the circumference of the top ring); then draw an arc from point D to point F (this is the circumference of the bottom ring). This gives the size of the shade. Add 0·6 cm ($\frac{1}{4}$ in.) for an overlapping join in the shade.

9 Join FE and continue the line. This should pass through point Z if the pattern is accurate.

10 Place a ruler between D and G and mark the centre. From this point place the ruler to Z and mark a grain line.

11 Cut out the pattern and try on rings. When

an accurate pattern has been obtained and the fit is satisfactory, cut out the lampshade fabric using the pattern, and noting the grain line.

12 Make up the shade using the method for the straight-sided drum shade on page 80.

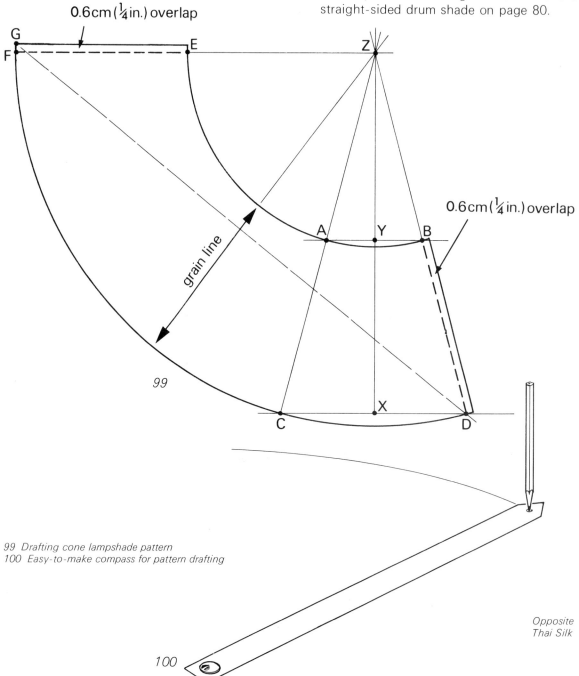

0.6cm ($\frac{1}{4}$ in.) overlap

0.6cm ($\frac{1}{4}$ in.) overlap

grain line

99 Drafting cone lampshade pattern
100 Easy-to-make compass for pattern drafting

Opposite
Thai Silk

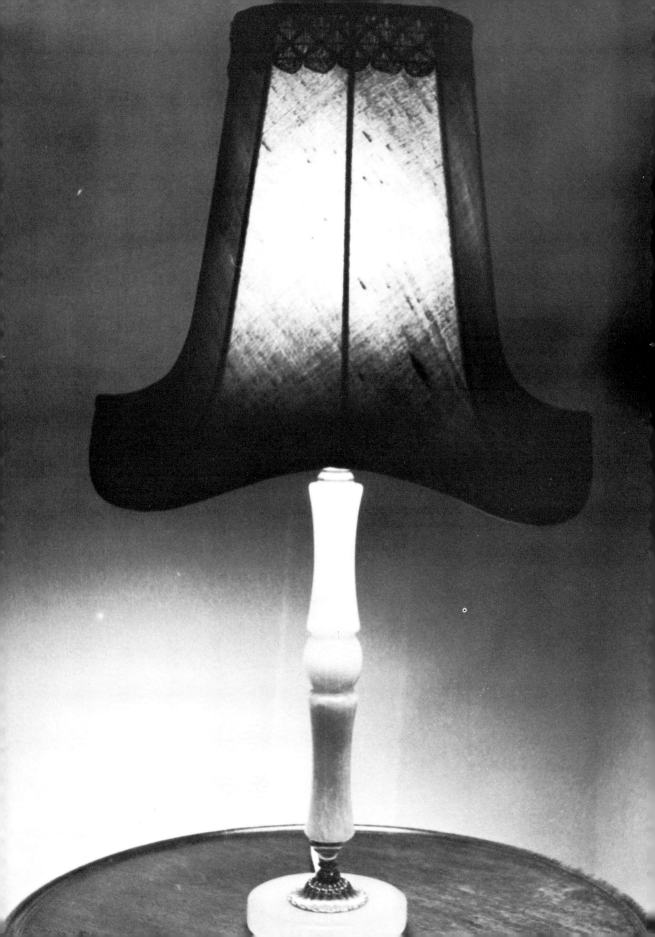

Suppliers

Lampshade frames, fabrics and trimmings, are obtainable from a number of craft shops and large stores, as well as from the following:

Frames and accessories	Fred Aldous Limited The Handicraft Centre PO Box 135 37 Lever Street Manchester M60 1UX
Trimmings	Distinctive Trimmings and Co Ltd 11 Marylebone Lane London W1 and 17 Church Street Kensington W8 The Lampshade Supply Service 21 Jerdan Place Fulham Broadway London SW6
Fabrics	Liberty Limited Regent Street London W1
Frames, fabrics, tape trimmings	John Lewis and Co Ltd Oxford Street London W1 and branches
Frames, fabrics for firm lampshades	M and F Products (Croydon) Limited Wandle Mills Bridle Path Beddington Croydon, Surrey
Frames, fabrics, trimmings	Nottingham Handcrafts Company (School Suppliers) Melton Road West Bridgford Nottingham NG2 6HD

Trimmings *Write for names of local stockists*	Rufflette Limited Chester Road Manchester M15 4JD
Fabrics, trimmings, tape	Russell Trading Company 75 Paradise Street Liverpool
Fabrics *Write for names of local stockists*	Arthur Sanderson Limited Berners Street London W1
	Southern Handicrafts George Street Hove, Sussex

INDEX